Broad Street and Beyond

Charleston's Historic Nexus of Power

by Margaret Middleton Rivers Eastman

and

Robert P. Stockton

Photography by Richard P. Donohoe

EVENING POST
BOOKS
Our Accent is Southern!

www.EveningPostBooks.com

Eastman, Margaret Middleton Rivers and Stockton, Robert P.
Broad Street: Charleston's Historic Nexus of Power

Published by Evening Post Books, Charleston, South Carolina.

ISBN-13: 978-1-929647-71-2

Interior design Michael J. Nolan

Cover design Michael J. Nolan, Peg Eastman, and Robert P. Stockton

Cover Image:

Broad Street viewed from St. Michael's steeple. Shepheard's Tavern building is clearly depicted on the left side of the image. Harbor forts — Castle Pinckney, Fort Sumter, and Fort Johnson are in background. St. Michael's steeple was used by the fire watch and Confederate lookouts. *Harper's Weekly* January 26, 1861.

Dedicated to Charlestonians

Margaret Simons Middleton, historian and preservationist

Margaret Middleton Rivers, author and loving mother

&

J. DeVeaux Stockton, Esq., a Broad Street lawyer

Acknowledgments

Charles Witte Waring, III, for permitting adaptation
of *Charleston Mercury* articles; managing editors
Emily Havener, Robert Salvo, and Prioleau Alexander

City of Charleston Mayor John Tecklenburg,
Elizabeth Bailey, and Mike Tito

Joseph P. Riley, Jr., Former City of Charleston Mayor

Vanessa Turner-Maybank, City of Charleston clerk of council

City of Charleston History Commission: Plus Philip Clapper.
Vanessa Ellington, Velvet Simmons

Amy Southerland and Daniel Riccio,
City of Charleston livability and tourism department

Leslie Wade, Charleston Parks Conservancy

Rabbi Stephanie Alexander and Anita Rosenberg, historian,
Kahal Kadosh Beth Elohim

Nicholas (Nic) Butler, historian; Lish Thompson,
Malcolm Hale, and Marianne Cawley, South Carolina Room,
Charleston County Library

Anne Cleveland, Charleston Library Society

Harlan Greene, Sam Stewart, and Catherine Stiers,
Marie (Ferrara) McGahan, College of Charleston, Addlestone Library,
Special Collections

John White, dean of libraries, College of Charleston Libraries

Bernard (Bernie) Powers, College of Charleston
Center for the Study of Slavery in Charleston

Jennifer McCormick, Carl Borick, Grahame Long
and Jennifer Scheetz, The Charleston Museum

Angela Mack, Amanda Breen, Deborah Nobles-McDaniel,
Sara Arnold, and Becky Heister, Gibbes Museum of Art

Renee Marshall and Katie Hyman, Huguenot Society of South Carolina

Bob Seidler, past chairman of the City of Charleston Tourism Commission

Alan Stello, Katherine Pemberton, and John Young,
Powder Magazine

Kristopher King, Evan Farmer, Andy Archie,
and Robert Gurley, Preservation Society of Charleston

Faye Jensen, Karen Stokes and Virginia Ellison, Lauren Nivens,
and Matthew Lockhart, South CarolinaHistorical Society

Tony Youmans, Old Exchange and Provost Dungeon

Eric Emerson, Bryan Collars, and Edwin Breeden,
South Carolina Department of Archives and History

Plus a myriad of friends who helped along the way:

Michael Allen, Elizabeth Alston, Dorothy Middleton Anderson,
Florence Anderson, Lee Ann Bain, Quentin Baxter, Mark Beck,
The Rev. Richard Belser, Eve Meddin Berlinsky, the late Rev. James Borum,
George and Lisa Bowen, Brian Boss, The Rev. Phillip C. Bryant,
Dr. C. (Chip) L. Bragg, Joseph (Bubber) Robert Cockrell Jr., Danny Crooks,
David DuBose, Robert G. Eastman, Lisa Farmer, Sarah Fick, Damon Fordham,
Dr. Sir Henry Fraser, K.A., Wilmot Fraser, Macky Hill, Langhorne Howard,
Catherine Jones, Harriott Pinckney Means Johnson,
Beverly Stoney Johnson, Alan Linkous, David McCormack, Suzie Marvin,
Philip A. Middleton, Brad Newman, Jola Newman, Marge Palmer,
Serge Polyachenko, Dan Ravenel, Charles J. Relyea Jr., James Rembert,
Mendel Rivers, Jr., Edna Cogswell Staubes Roberds, Robert Rosen,
Mickey Rosenblum, Anita Rosenberg, Margaret Seidler, Holmes Semken,
Randi Serrins, Carlton Simons, the late Thomas Grange Simons V,
Charles A. (Cal) Stephens, the late Theodore (Ted) Stern, Nancy Stockton,
Dale Theiling, Molly Thompson, Jane Thornhill Schachte,
Margaret von Werssowetz, Preston Wilson, and Rick Wilson

And last, but certainly not least, Pierre Manigault, John M. Burbage,
Michael Nolan, and Elizabeth Hollerith at Evening Post Books, Charleston, S.C.

Contents

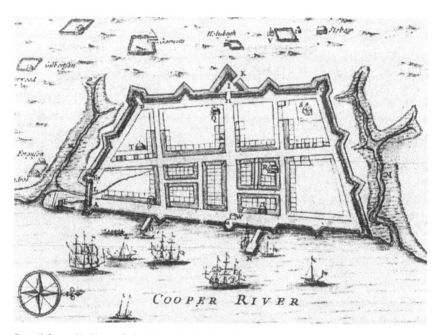

Detail from "A Plan of the Town & Harbor of Charles Town" insert for *A Compleat Description of the Province of Carolina in Three Parts* by Edward Crisp c 1710 Courtesy College of Charleston, Addlestone Library, Special Collections, Waddell Collection.

Introduction

This book celebrates Charleston's distinctive history, culture, and charm. It is a collection of true stories centered on, though not confined to, Broad Street, unquestionably Charleston's most historic thoroughfare.

Broad Street was intended to be the site of handsome public buildings, mercantile operations, and prestigious residences, and it has fulfilled that destiny. The street has been used for parades, public gatherings, and state funerals. It has been the scene of riots, duels, and various crimes. A custom house, banks, bars, lawyers, real estate companies, art shops, restaurants, churches, hotels, and other businesses have thrived there. Broad Street has served as the heartbeat of historic Charleston since the city's start on the peninsula in the 1670s.

In 2012, the American Planning Association selected Broad Street as one of the 10 Great Streets in America because of its rich colonial history, stunning 18th [and 19th] century architecture, and pedestrian orientation. The factual stories in this book support its conclusions.

The original plan for the city is known as The Grand Modell of Charles Town. It laid out the streets of the peninsula with Broad Street as the major east-west connector. More than thirty original settlers received grants for town lots along the avenue. They were a motley crowd, as might be expected. The focal point of the Grand Modell was an intersection, now Broad and Meeting streets, where a public square was drawn. The Charles Town plan was unique in that this was not to be an open square in the traditional sense. Important public structures were built on each point of the square, and today it is called the Four Corners of Law.

By 1704, a wall, disruptive though necessary, was constructed around most of the original town. It prevented a Franco-Spanish assault in 1706 and likely dissuaded an Indian attack during the Yemassee War in 1715. It figured in the rebellion against the Lords Proprietors in 1719. After the wall was torn down, the town gradually expanded west to the Ashley River marshes. Along the way, bombardment in two major wars, fires, tornadoes, hurricanes, and an earthquake brought major destruction, followed each time by rebuilding of both structures and lives by ever-resilient Charlestonians.

Safeguarding Charleston's cultural heritage occurred in earnest in 1920, decades before Americans elsewhere were thinking about historic preservation, when residents formed the Preservation Society of Charleston, the oldest such community-based organization in the nation. Largely because of the society's efforts, the city enacted the nation's first historic zoning ordinance in 1931.

This book is uniquely Charleston, ever changing yet somehow the same. The influence of the place and Charlestonians continues worldwide, and the city's charm remains captivating. Its mystique abounds in amazing stories, sights, smells, and sounds for all who care to experience its appeal. So, many thanks for joining us in this literary endeavor. Read at your leisure, and by all means enjoy!

"A view of Charles-Town, the capital of South Carolina," by Thomas Leitch, 1773, engraved by Samuel Smith, 1774, London. Courtesy Library of Congress.

Caroliniana

Colonization and Early History
of South Carolina

Barbadian Adventurers

To completely understand the settlement of the Carolina Province, one must be aware of upheavals that occurred on Barbados, the tiny, easternmost island of the West Indies in the Caribbean Sea. Barbados was settled by the English in 1625, and populated mostly by indentured laborers and a few landowners who exported cotton and tobacco.

With introduction of sugar cane from Brazil in the 1640s, the island's culture changed dramatically. Barbados became the richest English colony in North America. Sugar cane and its by-products — rum and molasses — were a lucrative cash crop. The allure of attainable wealth drew English adventurers to the island, and land values exploded. With little more than 100,000 acres of arable land, large estates displaced small holdings of the early settlers.

Map from Richard Ligon, Gent.'s book, *A True & Exact History of the Island of Barbadoes*, 1673.

In the 1640s when civil war raged in England, Barbados became an asylum for Royalists (Cavaliers) as well as Parliamentarians (Roundheads). They managed to live together amicably until King Charles I was beheaded in 1649. Parliament, then Oliver Cromwell,

"The Sugar Works," from Pierre Pomet, *A complete history of drugs.*
Published in Paris, 1694, republished in London, 1748.

took complete control of the English government and sought to bring the colony to heel by armed might and more restrictive laws.

When the monarchy was restored in 1660, Barbadian Royalists looked to the new king for reward for their loyalty and suffering. Charles II rewarded thirteen men with empty titles. One was John Colleton, who served as a colonel under his cousin Gen. John Berkeley, and after Cromwell's forces succeeded, fled to Barbados. In 1660, he joined another cousin, Gen. George Monck, with Anthony Ashley Cooper and others, in getting Charles II to the throne. Through John Berkeley's intervention, Colleton was knighted and appointed to the Council on Foreign Plantations, where he came in contact with some of the most powerful men in the realm.

The Province of Carolina

Colleton developed the idea of colonizing the vast wilderness between Virginia and Spanish Florida, and enlisted the support of his influential kinsmen, George Monck, now Duke of Albemarle, and John Berkeley, now Baron Berkeley of Stratton. Colleton later recruited Lord Chancellor Edward Hyde, Earl of Clarendon; William, Earl of Craven; Anthony Ashley Cooper (later Earl of Shaftesbury); Sir George Carteret of Jersey; and Sir William Berkeley, brother of John and governor of Virginia.

In 1663, King Charles II granted them a proprietary charter (revised in 1665) for the Province of Carolina. The paper empire gave them "Ecclesiastical and Civil" authority and included the lands south of Virginia to Spanish Florida, extending west to the Pacific Ocean. The king granted taxing and legislative powers, rights usually enjoyed by a ruling monarch.

Opportunities for making money seemed infinite. The Proprietors envisioned populating their holdings with experienced settlers from established colonies with promises of generous land grants and liberal political and religious rights. They expected colonists to bear the costs of colonizing and to compensate them through quit rents, a form of land tax.

News of the royal grant was welcomed in Barbados where land was already scarce. A group of planters formed the Corporation of Barbados Adventurers and sent out an expedition headed by Capt. William Hilton to find a site suitable for settlement. His travels identified a large island near the entrance to Port Royal Sound, and he named it "Hilton's Head" after himself. An account of his discoveries was published in London shortly after his return in 1664, but nothing came of his explorations.

The Ill-fated Cape Fear Colony

In 1663, to encourage settlement of their grant, the Proprietors signed an agreement with eighty-five Barbadian investors. A venture-capital company called "Adventurers for Carolina" was organized; members were to receive 500 acres for every 1,000 pounds of Muscovado sugar contributed. Newly knighted Sir John Yeamans was appointed governor of Cape Fear and authorized to establish a colony there.

Yeamans had impressive credentials. A sugar baron, he had owned land in Barbados since 1638. He served as a Royalist army colonel, and after Charles I was beheaded, immigrated to Barbados. Within ten years he became a large landholder and served as a militia colonel, judge and member of the Barbados Council.

Sir John and Lady Margaret Yeamans. Based on a drawing by Marjorie B. Hedges, this 20th century artwork has historical inaccuracies — Sir John's boot buckles are from the wrong era — but is charming nonetheless. Courtesy Yeamans Hall Club.

His personal life was messy. He had entered into a land partnership with Col. Benjamin Berringer and conducted an ill-concealed affair with his wife. According to public records she treated him so badly that Berringer would leave home and stay with friends. Berringer died in 1661. Governor William Lord Willoughby, in a 1668 report, accused Yeamans of poisoning Berringer "for no other reason but he had mind to the other gentleman's wife." Governor Willoughby's account contradicts the traditional tale that Yeamans killed Berringer in a duel. Yeamans married Margaret Berringer ten weeks later and moved into the Berringer home. Now called St. Nicholas Abbey, it is one of three remaining Jacobean mansions in the Western Hemisphere. In 1669 Colonel Berringer's children sued and were awarded ownership, forcing the Yeamans to relocate in Carolina.

Yeamans organized an expedition to establish a colony, to be called Charles Town in honor of the king, at Cape Fear. Bad luck plagued the expedition. One of Yeamans' three ships ran aground at the mouth of Cape Fear River, causing most of the provisions and arms to be lost. Yeamans returned to Barbados after authorizing Robert Sandford to explore the Carolina coast.

Sandford left a detailed account of his explorations. He encountered friendly Kiawah Indians at Edisto Island, and left Dr. Henry Woodward behind to learn their language. In exchange, Sandford took the chief's son with him to learn English ways, and promised to return. But Charles Town at Cape Fear was abandoned in 1667.

Anthony Ashley Cooper

In the early years of the Proprietorship, Sir John Colleton and his powerful cousin George, Duke of Albemarle, assumed leadership. Colleton died in 1666, and Albemarle retired from public life due to poor health. Then the Earl of Clarendon fell from power and fled into exile in 1667. With their numbers depleted, some Proprietors lost interest in Carolina.

The venture was rescued by Anthony Ashley Cooper, Lord Ashley. In 1669, although not yet Earl of Shaftesbury, his career was approaching its peak. He persuaded the Lords Proprietors to make significant investments in Carolina. Each agreed to contribute £500 sterling to start settlement and £200 for four years to support the colony.

Ashley moved quickly. Within three months he recruited more than 100 colonists, purchased and outfitted three ships (*Carolina, Port*

Royal and *Albemarle*), and appointed Capt. Joseph West to command the expedition. The fleet was ready to sail in August 1669.

Anthony Ashley Cooper, Earl of Shaftesbury, by Sir Peter Lely, published in W.D. Christie, *A Life of Anthony Ashley Cooper*, London, 1871. Broad Street was known as Cooper Street for a time.

The Proprietors expected the Carolina venture to be profitable, and wanted the province to be governed well. During the summer of 1669, the Fundamental Constitutions was written. According to tradition, Lord Ashley commissioned John Locke to write it. The Fundamental Constitutions was idealized as the foundation for a perfect society, namely an oligarchy ruled by a benevolent hierarchy of titled, wealthy, highly moral individuals who practiced the Anglican faith. The Fundamental Constitutions set up the division of land, protected slavery, and granted religious freedoms to all who professed to believe in God. The exception was Roman Catholics, who since Tudor times had been suspected of wanting to overthrow the Church of England and its head, the monarch. Though not specifically mentioned in the Fundamental Constitutions, it was "understood" that Catholics were not welcome.

On to Carolina

The Carolina expedition got off to a poor start. The ships stopped at Kinsale, Ireland, to pick up Capt. Florence O'Sullivan, who would be the chief military officer, and to recruit servants. Unfortunately, some settlers deserted at Kinsale. The ships finally reached Barbados in October and remained there until February. Authorized by the Proprietors, Sir John Yeamans named himself governor of the expedition. Before they sailed, a gale wrecked *Albemarle* and Yeamans hired *Three Brothers* as a replacement.

The sail to Carolina was a near disaster. The ships ran into a huge storm and scattered near the island of Nevis. *Port Royal* wrecked near Abaco in the Bahamas. Only *Carolina* and *Three Brothers* landed in Bermuda, where some of *Port Royal*'s survivors managed to rejoin them. Yeamans left the expedition and William Sayle, the eighty-year-old former governor of Bermuda, replaced him.

On the voyage from Bermuda, another storm drove *Three Brothers* to Virginia. Only the 200-ton frigate *Carolina* landed at Bull's Island, some thirty miles north of present-day Charleston. The Proprietors had originally intended to settle in Port Royal, but the cacique of the Kiawah Indians met the landing party and, on his advice, *Carolina* proceeded to Albemarle Point on the west bank of the Ashley River, landing in April 1670.

Churchmen and Dissenters

To populate the colony quickly, the Lords Proprietors encouraged settlers of diverse religious faiths. The 1663 Carolina charter directed the Proprietors to "indulge" any inhabitants who "cannot in their private opinions, conform to ... the Church of England."

The Fundamental Constitutions also guaranteed liberty of conscience to all who professed a belief in God.

Mary Fisher Cross, a Quaker preacher, was known as "she that spake to the great Turk," after her unsuccessful attempt in 1658 to convert Ottoman Sultan Mehmed IV. She settled in Charles Town in 1675 and was one of the largest landowners on Broad Street. Engraving from William Cullen Bryant's *Popular History*, 1881.

Under these provisions, Carolina attracted Jews, who were in the province by 1695. There were also Carolina slaves who observed Muslim prayer, diet and fasting.

However, the chief benefactors of Carolina's religious liberty were Dissenters, or Nonconformists. They were Protestants who did not conform to religious beliefs and practices of the Church of England, and included Baptists, French Protestants (Huguenots), Quakers, Presbyterians, Congregationalists, and Lutherans.

By 1680, Church of England men (Churchmen) and Dissenters were about equal in the population. But the politically powerful "Goose Creek Men," mostly Churchmen from Barbados, opposed the Proprietors' efforts to regulate trade, collect quit-rents, and prevent enslavement of Indians.

To dilute the Churchmen's power, the Proprietors encouraged immigration of Dissenters and promoted their interests. Dissenters filled appointive offices and their leaders became landgraves. The Commons House of Assembly often was dominated by Churchmen, but sometimes Dissenters held the majority.

In the mid-1690s, when Dissenters had a majority, they overstepped in a way that alienated their best supporters, the Lords Proprietors. They sought to deprive the French Huguenots of their civil rights and even tried to prevent them from bequeathing land to their children, when only property owners could vote and serve in office. The Lords Proprietors disallowed the measures against the Huguenots. The Alien Act of 1697 guaranteed liberty of conscience and the rights of Englishmen to French Protestants and Jews. Huguenots, in retaliation against the Dissenters, allied with the Churchmen.

Establishment was a hot issue. The Fundamental Constitutions had called for establishment of the Church of England. The Dissenters, who remembered the Church in England as an instrument of suppression, opposed the Fundamental Constitutions for that reason, and the document was never ratified.

1706, the Assembly had Churchmen and Huguenots in the majority. They enacted the Church Act of 1706, establishing the Church of England as the state church. Ten parishes were created, in which churches and rectories were to be built with tax money. Additional parishes were created as needed. Many parishes had the same names as Barbadian parishes, such as St. Philip and St. Michael.

In 1716, Church parishes were designated as civic units for election of Assembly members. The parish electoral system persisted until 1865. Parishes also were public school and welfare agencies. Because parishes had secular functions, Dissenters could serve on vestries.

The Dissenters played a valuable role in the early settlement of the Carolina colony.

Landgraves, Caciques and Baronies

The Lords Proprietors of Carolina, in their Fundamental Constitutions of Carolina, established a colonial nobility with generous land grants to sustain them. The grants, entitled seignories and baronies, each contained 12,000 acres. The acreage did not have to be contiguous.

At the top were the Proprietors, who held a seigniory in each county. Over time, seignories came to be called baronies. For example, Lord Ashley's Seigniory of St. Giles on the Ashley River became known as Ashley Barony.

Below the Proprietors were landgraves and caciques (cassiques). Sewee Barony, in the vicinity of Awendaw Creek, was assigned to Governor Sir Nathaniel Johnson when he became a landgrave in 1703. John Smith, who became a cacique in 1682, received as part of his patent 6,000 acres on the Pon Pon (Edisto) River.

The term barony has caused confusion, as no barons were created.

The colonial noble titles were not to be equated with the English peerage, which is why non-English titles were used. Landgrave came from a German title, *landgraf*, equivalent to a count. Cacique came from a Spanish term, *cacique*, for Indian chief.

Lowcountry Slavery

Enslaved labor was encouraged from the outset of the Carolina colony. Four of the Lords Proprietors were members of the Royal African Company, a slave-trading enterprise, and Barbadian settlers brought with them a plantation culture complete with a harsh slave code. Settlers were promised twenty acres for every African male and ten acres for every African female brought to the colony.

Imported Africans were first quarantined on Sullivan's Island to ensure that they brought no sickness into the city. The first "pest house" was built around 1707; in 1796, it was moved to Fort Johnson on James Island.

Charleston was the primary import port during the colonial and early national periods, and the slave trade was the most lucrative component of international maritime trade. An estimated 400,000

The Old Plantation, by John Rose, South Carolina, ca. 1790. Dancers performing with West African instruments – *shegureh* (woman's rattle made from calabash), banjo and drum. Abby Aldrich Rockefeller Folk Art Museum, Williamsburg, Virginia.

Africans were brought to the United States before the international slave trade was outlawed in 1807. Of those, about forty per cent, nearly 160,000, came into Charleston.

Slaves were sold at the public auction ground on the north side of the Exchange building until 1856, when City Council outlawed the outdoor sale of slaves. Slave auctions also were held in private establishments such as William Payne & Sons, operating at 32-34 Broad Street from 1803 to 1834.

The Charles Town Triangle

Henry Laurens and his London partner controlled a triangular trade connecting Charles Town with England and Sierra Leone on the Rice Coast of West Africa. Laurens would ship South Carolina products to Richard Oswald in London. Oswald would ship guns and other trade goods to Sierra Leone. Guns were crucial cargo as they were used in the capture of slaves. Oswald's firm owned a slave "factory" or "castle" on Bunce Island, strategically situated in the Sierra Leone River near Freetown, capital of the colony. Captives

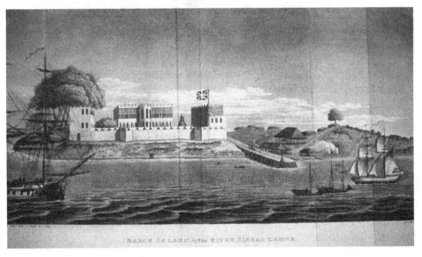

"Slave factory" on Bunce Island. Engraving from a painting by Joseph Corry, 1805. Archaeology on-site indicates Corry's depiction was more fanciful than accurate. Courtesy Gilder Lehman Institute, Yale University.

were brought to the fortified factory where they were kept until ready for shipment. The factory included slave houses, warehouses for supplies, and a luxurious home for the company agent. Captives were loaded onto slave ships at Bunce Island for shipment to Charles Town, where they were sold by Laurens.

A slave father sold away from his family, frontispiece of *The Child's Anti-Slavery Book*, New York, 1860. Courtesy Library of Congress.

No social stigma attached to the slave trade, only profit. Mansions such as the elegant Miles Brewton House at 27 King Street were built with fortunes from the slave trade. Laurens was a respected Patriot leader in the American Revolution and was elected president of the Continental Congress. Christopher Gadsden was leader of the Sons of Liberty, while owning Gadsden's Wharf, the largest slave importation depot in North America.

The agricultural economy of South Carolina was dependent upon enslaved labor. Rice was the primary export, and slaves from the Rice Coast were considered the most valuable because of their unique skills; rice had been grown in their homeland for centuries. They brought with them West African traditions, from planting methods to hoeing in unison to work songs.

Lowcountry agriculture was organized on the task system in which slaves were assigned individual tasks such as clearing, hoeing, digging ditches etc. When finished with their tasks, workers were given time to grow food on allotted land known as Negro plots. The vegetable plots benefitted the plantation owner, whose expenses were reduced, and benefitted workers who had a healthier traditional African diet of beans and greens. This production method was less brutal than the gang system practiced elsewhere.

Auction advertisement from the *South-Carolina Gazette*. Courtesy Library of Congress.

But slaves still were slaves. Dissatisfaction with their condition often was expressed by running away. From 1732, when the *South-Carolina Gazette* was established, until 1865, newspapers ran advertisements for the return of runaways. The legal right of owners to retrieve runaways was written into the U.S. Constitution as the Fugitive Slave Clause.

Stono Rebellion

In 1739 word reached the province that war had broken out between England and Spain. South Carolina authorities began building up Charles Town's fortifications, and increased vigilance.

In September the Stono Rebellion erupted. It is believed the rebels were inspired by a Spanish offer of freedom to any enslaved person who succeeded in fleeing the English colonies. The rebellion began near the Stono River when rebels broke into Hutchinson's Store and murdered the white men in charge. They took guns and ammunition and began marching toward Florida. They killed whites, burned houses, confiscated guns and recruited or coerced slaves to join the march. The only white spared was a Mr. Wallace, tavern keeper at Rantowles, known to be kind to blacks.

The rebels were intercepted and subdued after they stopped to rest near the Pon Pon (Edisto) River. Few escaped. Leaders were tried and executed and others severely punished. Those who had been forced to join were pardoned. The slave code was strengthened with harsher penalties.

Denmark Vesey's Failed Insurrection

Denmark Vesey had been enslaved in the Caribbean before he arrived in Charleston belonging to Capt. Joseph Vesey. In 1799 he won a city lottery and bought his freedom. Vesey picked up his lottery winnings at the Exchange, which was then City Hall. Although free, his life was subject to legal restrictions as free persons of color were viewed with suspicion by white authorities.

According to court records, Vesey plotted a rebellion scheduled for Bastille Day, July 14, 1822. He and his followers planned to execute slave owners, liberate the enslaved, and sail to Haiti to escape retaliation. But the plan was revealed by Peter, a house servant belonging to Col. John Cordes Prioleau. The militia was called out and 313 suspects were arrested. Sixty-seven were convicted, and Vesey and thirty-four others were hanged near Line Street.

St. Philip's vestry reported to the congregation that "not one belonging to the Episcopal Church having been found in the ranks of the Insurgents, but the colored man (belonging to Mr. Prioleau) who gave information of the plot was of the Association of this Church."

After the Vesey plot, laws governing the movements of slaves and free blacks were made more stringent. Enslaved individuals who worked outside their owners' property had to wear badges identifying them by number and occupation. Because of the fear that slaves might be influenced by abolitionist material, it was made unlawful to teach them to read and write.

Enslaved people were prohibited by law from meeting without white supervision, including religious services. Enslaved and free persons of color sat in galleries of Charleston churches during services. In the 1860s, there was a mass movement of black worshipers to establish their own churches. Tradition recalls a white church leader urging black communicants to continue worshiping in their galleries, to which a Northern missionary is said to have responded, "There are no galleries in Heaven."

The Work House

The Work House on Magazine Street was a place to punish enslaved individuals accused of infractions. The building, designed by architect Edward C. Jones in the Romanesque Revival style, was begun in 1850. The City collected fees from slave owners for punishments, which included whipping and walking

The Work House. Courtesy College of Charleston, Addlestone Library, Waddell Collection.

on a treadmill. There also was a slave mart in the yard. Because of the inhumane conditions, dozens of inmates used stakes and pickaxes to escape. Later apprehended, the trial on Bastille Day 1849 was downplayed by contemporaries, and this historical event is only now coming to light in a book by Jeff Strickland entitled *All for Liberty*.

The Work House was closed by Union authorities in 1865, and afterwards was a hospital for African Americans. It was damaged by the 1886 Earthquake and razed. The horrors of the Work House were referenced in the 2018 City of Charleston resolution apologizing for slavery.

Gains, Losses, Renewal and Hope

Slavery was abolished by the 13th Amendment in 1865, voting rights for black men were legalized by the 15th Amendment, and additional civil rights ensured by Congressional acts and the South Carolina state constitution of 1868. After 1876, however, Federal guarantees began to erode as Southern whites returned to power. The state constitution of 1895 and Jim Crow laws curtailed black voting and other civil rights.

Black citizens were excluded from voting in the Democratic Primary, at a time when it was South Carolina's de facto election, until 1948, when federal Judge J. Waties Waring opened the party's rolls to black voters. Clarendon County's 1951 *Briggs v. Elliott* case was bundled with others for the U.S. Supreme Court's 1954 landmark *Brown v. The Board of Education of Topeka, Kansas*, that desegregated public schools. The decision opened the doors to desegregation of other public facilities, hotels and restaurants. The Voting Rights Act of 1965 again guaranteed voting rights.

The massacre of innocents by Dylan Roof at Emanuel AME Church in 2015 was meant to incite racial strife. It had the opposite effect as blacks and whites united to walk across the Ravenel Bridge in an unparalleled display of racial harmony. The general outcry was so great that it influenced legislators to remove the Confederate flag from the State House grounds. Significant progress has been made in civil rights since the 1950s. Yet the challenge to hold onto hard-won rights in an adversarial world remains. Charleston's new International African American Museum is expected to be a monumental achievement that not only chronicles the past, but also offers great hope for the future.

Wily Sir Nathaniel

In 1701, the War of the Spanish Succession began in Europe. In the colonies, it was known as Queen Anne's War. The English opposed the placement on the Spanish throne of Philip V, a grandson of the French King Louis XIV, as an increase in France's power. The war affected provincial Carolina because the French were now allied with Spain, and the Spanish presence in Florida was a constant threat.

Formal notification of hostilities arrived in Charles Town, and the Assembly voted to send an expedition to capture St. Augustine in Florida. Gov. James Moore led a force that burned the town, but were unable to take the fort that guarded the harbor. Spanish reinforcements eventually forced the Carolinians to withdraw, and the expedition did not eliminate the Spanish threat.

Gov. Sir Nathaniel Johnson, dated 1705, by an unidentified artist. Courtesy Gibbes Museum of Art/Carolina Art Association.

Such was the political climate when Sir Nathaniel Johnson replaced Governor Moore in 1703. The new governor was from Kibblesworth, County Durham. He had served in Parliament and the Army. As a loyal follower of the Stuarts, he was knighted and appointed governor of the Leeward Islands in 1686. When James II was deposed two years later, he was removed from office for refusing to swear allegiance to sovereigns William and Mary.

Sir Nathaniel obtained permission to retire in Carolina where he had large grants of land on the eastern branch of the Cooper River. He arrived in 1689 with the title of cacique, and later became a landgrave. He experimented with silk culture and encouraged planters to cultivate rice. Johnson was quite popular because of his military experience. His main plantation fittingly was called Silk Hope.

In 1702, the Lords Proprietors appointed Johnson governor of South and North Carolina (the two parts of Carolina had evolved separately).

With war on the horizon, Johnson reorganized the militia and extended the city wall. The existing masonry wall and bastions along the Cooper were strengthened. Newly-built land portions consisted of earthworks with palisades on top and a moat. The slopes of the earthworks and moat were lined with logs. All of this was state-of-the-art at the time. Johnson had observed such earthworks by French military engineer Sebastien de Vauban and their effectiveness in Louis XIV's wars against his neighbors.

Johnson had a fort built on Windmill Point on James Island (now Fort Johnson) and a guard was stationed on Sullivan's Island. In 1706 he outfitted a privateer to cruise near Havana. On August 24 the privateer rushed back with news that he was being chased by five French vessels carrying French and Spanish soldiers. The enemy commander had learned that Charles Town was suffering from a yellow fever epidemic and assumed that the town was vulnerable.

Word was sent to Governor Johnson at Silk Hope, and Col. William Rhett summoned the militia. The governor and men from outlying areas arrived the following day and encamped about a half mile beyond the city walls to avoid the epidemic. A signal from Sullivan's Island warned of the approaching fleet. The French ships sailed across the bar, but turned back when they saw the city's fortifications, and anchored near Sullivan's Island.

The following morning a French emissary came under a flag of truce. At Granville Bastion, he was blindfolded, led into the fort and met with the governor. Wily Sir Nathaniel had him blindfolded again while he was escorted from bastion to bastion to see the defenses. What the envoy did not realize was that the same militiamen would dash to the next location before he arrived, thus making the fortifications seem well manned. In spite of this show of force, the Frenchman demanded that the governor surrender. Johnson flatly refused. Believing that the town was prepared for a frontal assault, the French sent marauding parties into outlying areas.

On James Island, friendly Indians had been organized and rushed screaming through the woods, causing invaders to flee. A raiding party on Wando Neck, feasting on stolen cattle and pigs, were surprised by militiamen. Many intruders were killed or taken prisoner as they fled to their boats and went out to sea.

Rhett, appointed vice admiral, commanded six hastily armed vessels. Word came that a French ship with 200 armed men aboard was moored north of Charles Town in Sewee Bay. Rhett sailed out the following day, while land forces killed fourteen and took fifty prisoners. Surprised, the invaders never fired a shot.

Their commander offered a ransom of 10,000 pieces of eight and hastily sailed away, leaving behind 230 prisoners, mostly Florida Indians who were sold as slaves. This victory suspended the Spanish threat.

Broughton's Failed Coup d'Etat

Gov. Johnson was replaced by Edward Tynte in November 1709. But Tynte's death the following June almost caused a civil war.

In the event of a governor's death, only a duly-appointed Proprietor's deputy could assume the governorship until the Proprietors selected a successor. When Tynte died, three Proprietors' deputies were living in the province: Thomas Broughton, deputy to John, Baron Carteret, and a member of the Grand Council; Chief Justice and Landgrave Robert Gibbes, deputy of Sir John Colleton, Baronet; and Fortesque Turbeville, the recently arrived deputy of Henry, Duke of Beaufort, the Craven heir. Before dying, Tynte instructed them to choose one of their number as governor.

View of Mulberry, House and Street, ca. 1800, by Thomas Coram. Courtesy Gibbes Museum of Art/Carolina Art Association.

Broughton had a checkered past. He had married Nathaniel Johnson's daughter before emigrating from the West Indies in the 1690s. With Johnson as governor, Broughton tried to secure a monopoly of the Indian trade. The Assembly declined his offer. Broughton continued to try to dominate the trade and in 1708 was prosecuted by Indian agent Thomas Nairne on charges that he had enslaved friendly Cherokees and misappropriated 1,000 deerskins belonging to the province. Governor Johnson had his son-in-law acquitted and had Nairne arrested for treason on dubious charges.

Broughton used his privileged position to obtain the lucrative office of surveyor general. His country seat was Mulberry, on the western branch of Cooper River, and he was part of the Goose Creek Men, the political elite of the colony.

Robert Gibbes immigrated from Barbados in 1672. His association with the Proprietors helped his political rise. He owned extensive acreage along the Cooper and was a member of the Goose Creek faction, although one of its moderates.

The three deputies met, voted for a governor and recessed. They reconvened in the afternoon, and Gibbes was proclaimed governor. It was later "discovered" that Broughton had received a two-to-one vote in the morning, and Gibbes was accused of bribing Turbeville to change his vote during the recess. In the midst of the controversy, Turbeville died suddenly, and some claimed he had been poisoned.

The Attempted Coup

Incensed at losing the election, Broughton assembled supporters at Mulberry and marched to Charles Town to claim the governorship. Governor Gibbes, who lived in town, heard of Broughton's approach and ordered the drawbridge at Johnson's Ravelin hauled up.

Broughton reached the ravelin, demanding admittance. Gibbes inquired why Broughton and his men were armed and if they acknowledged him as governor. "We have understood," they answered, "that there is an alarm about something or other in the town, and have come to see what is the matter." During this interchange, some of Broughton's militia had galloped towards Craven's Bastion to gain entrance, but quickly returned when they were unsuccessful.

A detail from the 1711 Edward Crisp Map illustrates Johnson's Ravelin, a triangular fortification at Broad and Meeting streets, the main land entrance. Johnson's Ravelin (I) the city gate (K) and the drawbridge across the moat (H) are depicted. Courtesy Walled City Task Force.

Meanwhile, some sailors tried to force down the drawbridge. Gibbes did not allow his men to fire upon them. Consequently, the sailors and Broughton's men managed to lower the bridge.

Broughton's men proceeded down Broad Street to the Watch House, where two companies of the militia were armed and waiting. One of Broughton's men drew a proclamation from his pocket and tried to read it. The governor's militia made such racket with drums and shouts that no syllable could be heard.

A sailor grabbed the militia colors, and tore them from the staff. A few militiamen opened fire but nobody was hurt. A militia captain drew his sword, stepped up to the sailor, and demanded the torn flag. Prudently, one of Broughton's men alighted, and made the sailor return it. Then the hotheads withdrew to a tavern to read their proclamation a second time and enjoy exuberant toasts.

Broughton agreed to a compromise that permitted Gibbes to remain acting governor until the Proprietors selected a replacement. During the early months of Gibbes' administration, the Assembly refused to form a quorum in protest to the irregularity of his election. Ultimately, the Proprietors declared Gibbes' election illegal because of bribery and refused to pay his salary. They chose neither contender, appointing as governor Charles Craven, younger brother of Proprietor William, Baron Craven.

After the attempted coup, Broughton returned to Goose Creek and acquired more land. In spite of the fact that he had been the colony's surveyor general, in 1715 he built Mulberry Castle on land that belonged to Sir Peter Colleton. When the irregularity was discovered, he had to trade Colleton 300 acres and £150 to secure the site of his residence. He held numerous offices afterwards including interim governor after his brother-in-law Robert Johnson died in 1735. According to historians, Broughton's administration was rank with discord and marred by maladministration.

Truth is...

Governor Gibbes died in 1715, and history primarily remembers his disputed election. This defamation may be unfounded. Turbeville had just arrived, and during the recess, the chief justice may have acquainted him with some of Broughton's questionable business practices. Turbeville's subsequent death may have been coincidental, as many newcomers did not adjust well to the colony's climate and some died of unknown maladies. It is interesting to note that Broughton discovered the voting anomaly "later."

The Bloodless Revolution of 1719

The Lords Proprietors ruled the colony for more than a half century. The initial Proprietors promoted good government, religious harmony, and protection of the civil rights of Dissenters, Huguenots, and Jews. But by 1719 only three of the original Proprietary shares were still owned by heirs of Craven, Carteret, and Colleton.

The later Proprietors were less idealistic. They did not respect Dissenters, raised the quit rents, and tried to limit the Assembly's power. During the Yemassee War in 1715-17, the Proprietors provided no military aid and even turned down a Crown offer of funding. Afterwards, they claimed the abandoned Yemassee lands for themselves.

South Carolinians petitioned the Crown to take over the Province. The movement gained powerful political support and in November 1719, members of the Assembly informed Gov. Robert Johnson that they "would have no Proprietors' Government," and asked him to govern in the name of King George I. Johnson, having been appointed by the Proprietors, felt obligated by his oath to them and refused. In December the Assembly declared itself to be a "Convention of the People" governing in the king's name.

Col. James Moore II, son of former Gov. James Moore and a hero of the Yemassee War, was appointed governor by the Convention and served until 1721. Governor Johnson tried to rally the militia to his side, but failed. Charles Town's fortifications had been taken over by militiamen loyal to the Convention. Col. William Rhett, whom the Lords Proprietors had appointed to the lucrative posts of receiver general and comptroller of customs, was one of the few prominent men opposed to the takeover. The revolution was practically bloodless.

Col. William Rhett, pastel by Henrietta De Beau-
lieu Deering Johnston, ca. 1710. Courtesy Gibbes
Museum of Art/Carolina Art Association.

The Convention then resolved itself to be the Commons House of Assembly. Petitions were addressed to George I and the Board of Trade, requesting that South Carolina become a Crown colony. The Crown readily agreed. However, the Proprietors resisted, and a protracted court battle ensued. Finally, in 1729, seven of the eight Proprietors sold their shares to the Crown.

Francis Nicholson, a former soldier who had served in several colonial administrative posts, was appointed as the King's governor of South Carolina in 1721. Nicholson brought in royal troops to protect the province, and the HMS *Scarborough*, commanded by Capt. George Anson, was assigned to Charles Town.

The Lords Proprietors, as part of their case, put forward false accusations perpetrated by Rhett and others that Governor Nicholson was guilty of smuggling and cooperating with the Spanish. In

1725, he returned to London to clear his name. The Crown did not take the accusations seriously and promoted him to lieutenant-general. However, Nicholson died in London in 1729.

Arthur Middleton, who had been president of the Convention, served as acting governor from 1725 to 1730. Robert Johnson, "the pirate hunter" who had opposed the Revolution of 1719, was appointed governor in 1730. Prior to his arrival, to ensure that the interest of the province was closest to his heart, Johnson disposed of his patrimony in England.

Johnson, known as "the Good Governor," remained in office until his death in 1735. A grateful town honored him with the first state funeral held in the colony and his peers erected a large marble memorial enumerating his virtues in St. Philip's Church. Unfortunately, the memorial was destroyed when the church burned in 1835.

Near this Place lyes the Body of his Excellency/ROBERT JOHNSON, Esquire/His Majesty's/First Captain General, Governor and Commander/in Chief and Vice-Admiral of this Province,/After the Purchase thereof from the/Lords Proprietors./Who Dyed the 3d day of May/Annoque Domini 1735, aged 58 years./To whose Memory The General Assembly gave/ This Marble to be Erected as a Mark of Peculiar/Esteem and Gratitude for his Mild, Just/and Generous Administration./ And beside him lyes his Beloved Consort,/Mrs. MARGARET JOHNSON, an amiable, sensible Lady,/Of Exemplary Piety, Charity and Oeconomy,/Who Dyed the 5th day of July/Annoque Domini 1732, aged 45 years.

A House for VIPs

110 Broad Street was the residence of several notables. It was part of an ongoing pattern of wealthy Charlestonians living in historic houses ("houses their grandfathers built") noticed by a visitor from New York in the 1850s. Courtesy Library of Congress.

William Harvey's mansion at 110 Broad Street, built ca. 1728, proclaimed his prosperity as a merchant and planter and demonstrates upward mobility in the early colony. A 1715 deed identified William Harvey as a butcher, but in his will he called himself a "gentleman." Harvey built his new house after selling the nearby Lining house.

The house was designed for gracious living and for dances held in the drawing room in the era when Charleston was in its heyday. The floor plan is asymmetrical with four rooms on each of three floors. Scrutiny of the façade indicates that the center window on the ground floor was the original main entrance door, opening directly into the rectangular reception room. Later, this was considered indecorous and the main entrance was moved to the present location, with a new Adamesque doorway, entering into the smaller front room, which functions as a foyer. A stairway was located in the back. Another noteworthy exterior feature is the delicate iron balcony that is accessed from the drawing room. The drawing room could be expanded by opening wide hinged doors to the smaller parlor on the west.

Masonry outbuildings include a two-story kitchen/wash kitchen. The kitchen has a massive central chimney containing an eye-level bake oven with an arched iron door. The oven design was copied for the restoration of the Heyward-Washington House kitchen at 87 Church Street in 1929.

The carriage house/double stable building is in the Picturesque Gothic style. Two large "necessaries" were located in the northwest corner of the lot. In one was a miniature fireplace. A large, above-ground cistern was located near the kitchen. Rainwater was filtered into a catch basin and a wooden pump lifted water to ground level.

The Izards

The house had several prominent occupants. For six years, it was rented to Gov. James Glen, who had the longest tenure of any governor during the colonial period (1743-1756). Glen is noted for stressing royal prerogative in the face of persistent challenge from the Commons House of Assembly and for his role in Indian affairs. He was also known for the humanity shown to Acadian deportees from Nova Scotia who unexpectedly arrived in the province in 1755.

After Governor Glen left, Benjamin Harvey, son of the builder, sold the house to a well-connected Goose Creek planter, Ralph Izard. Born at The Elms in St. James, Goose Creek,

Parish, he was a son of Henry Izard and Margaret Johnson. His maternal grandfather was the "pirate hunter," Gov. Robert Johnson.

Young Izard pursued classical studies in England and returned to America briefly in 1764. He took up residence in London in 1771 and later moved to Paris. The Continental Congress appointed him commissioner to the Court of Tuscany in 1776. He returned to America in 1780, leaving his family in France. Active in the Revolutionary cause, he was a member of the Continental Congress and pledged his large estate for the payment of warships.

After the Revolution, Izard was elected to the U.S. Senate and served as president pro tempore during the Third Congress. He was one of the founders of the College of Charleston. Izard died in 1804 and was buried at St. James, Goose Creek, Parish Church.

Ralph Izard and his wife Alice Delancey (of a prominent New York family) are portrayed in a portrait by John Singleton Copley. Painted in London in 1775, it now hangs at the Boston Museum of Fine Arts.

Burning of the frigate *Philadelphia* in the harbor of Tripoli. Courtesy Library of Congress.

Their son Ralph Delancey Izard volunteered in 1804 for Lt. Stephen Decatur's attempt to destroy the USS *Philadelphia* after she had run aground on a reef near Tripoli and the Barbary Pirates had towed the scuttled boat into the harbor. In an audacious night-time raid, the Americans slipped into the harbor and managed to burn her. Lord Horatio Nelson called the naval assault "the most bold and daring act of the Age." The destroyer USS *Izard*, commissioned in 1942, was named in Izard's honor.

Another son, Maj. Gen. George Izard, served with distinction in the War of 1812. He was later governor of Arkansas, where Izard County was named for him. As a young Army officer in the 1790s, he had supervised the construction of Castle Pinckney in Charleston harbor.

Descendant Ralph Stead Izard sold 110 Broad Street to his uncle and aunt, Joel Roberts and Mary Poinsett. She was the widow of John Julius Pringle and the granddaughter of Ralph Izard.

Joel Roberts Poinsett

Poinsett was another of Charleston's distinguished statesmen. He was born in Charleston in 1779, a son of Dr. Elisha Poinsett, a wealthy physician and landowner, and Katherine Ann Roberts, an Englishwoman. He benefitted from his family's wealth and his mother's social connections. He spent his early childhood in England and was educated in Connecticut and London. He studied medicine at the University of Edinburgh and attended the military school in Woolwich, England.

Poinsett traveled in Europe and the Middle East from 1801 to 1809. His travels brought him to the Court of Russia, where Czar Alexander I tried to recruit him for his civil service. In Geneva, he was the guest of Madame de Stael, the celebrated woman of letters and political theorist, and her father Jacques Necker, former finance minister of France. In the Khanate of

Kuban, he negotiated for the return of stolen horses, persuading the Khan that the theft would reflect badly on his country's image.

Because he spoke Spanish, President James Madison appointed him counsel general in 1809, and sent him to Argentina and Chile to assess their struggle for independence from Spain, and to negotiate trade agreements. Poinsett remained in South America until 1814, then returned to Charleston.

In 1817, he was elected to the state House of Representatives and to the U.S. House in 1825, serving to 1829. He was a staunch Unionist during the Nullification Crisis in 1832-33.

President Martin Van Buren chose Poinsett as secretary of war in 1837. In that position, he made improvements at West Point, engaged a French scientist to study flora and fauna of the American West, and oversaw a naval expedition in the Pacific that returned with valuable scientific information.

President James Monroe appointed Poinsett as a special envoy to newly independent Mexico in 1822-23. He returned to Mexico as minister plenipotentiary and in 1829 signed the first treaty recognizing the boundary between the U. S. and Mexico. Poinsett tried unsuccessfully to negotiate the purchase of northern Mexican territories including California and New Mexico. (The United States gained most of those territories as a result of the Mexican War in 1845-48.)

Poinsett was elected a fellow of the American Academy of Arts and Sciences in 1825. He was a co-founder in 1840 of the National Institution for the Promotion of Science and the Useful Arts, a forerunner of the Smithsonian Institution. Poinsett is best known for a plant he brought back from Mexico and propagated in Charleston, the poinsettia.

Poinsett story contributed by Catherine Jones.

Euphorbia pulcherrima, Poinsettia. Courtesy Library of Congress. The Mexican name for the poinsietta is *Flor de la Noche Buena* (Christmas Flower) and it became a seasonal fixture in the United States.

The King Family

In 1858, the Poinsetts sold the Broad Street house to Judge Mitchell King, municipal judge, trustee, and interim president of the College of Charleston. King founded the Philosophical Society of Charleston and authored treatises on scientific and agricultural subjects.

The property remained in the King family for many years. One member was George D. Bryan, who married Judge King's daughter Mary Middleton King. Bryan was a son of United States District Judge George Seabrook Bryan and Rebecca Louisa Dwight.

After the war, Bryan returned to Charleston and practiced law. In 1878, he became the city's legal counsel and was elected mayor in 1887 in an uncontested race. In 1894, President Grover Cleveland appointed him collector of customs in Charleston, a job he held until 1898. He was a probate judge from December 1901 until he died at his home in 1919. The house remained in the family until the death of his great-niece Miss Rebecca Bryan in 1976.

110 Broad Street Privy. Courtesy Library of Congress.

St. Michael's Church

The first Church of England in the colony was built on the southeast corner of the public square at the intersection now known as the Four Corners of Law. Called St. Philip's Church, it was built ca. 1682. The first St. Philip's was wrecked by a storm in 1710, and the second was completed in the 1720s on upper Church Street. The design was similar to what was *au courant* in London.

St. Michael's Church. Courtesy Library of Congress.

Architectural historians agree that the second St. Philip's Church was the finest ecclesiastical building built in colonial British North America. It was the first church in the colonies to have a steeple, and the first to have a classical portico — and not just one but three. The triple porticos may have been inspired by the multiple porticos of Andrea Palladio's Villa Rotunda.

The second St. Philip's is the only known colonial building to be pictured in a contemporary European magazine. In England, statesman and aesthete Edmund Burke described St. Philip's as "spacious and executed in a very handsome taste, exceeding everything of that kind which we have in America."

St. Philip's Church, *Gentlemen's Magazine*, June 1753. Courtesy College of Charleston, Addlestone Library, Special Collections, Waddell Collection.

In the thirty-year interim between the completion of the second St. Philip's Church and 1751, Charles Town had become the third largest city in British North America, surpassed only by Boston and Philadelphia. It had grown so much that the South Carolina government was prepared to build a new set of public buildings. Among them was a new Anglican church that would ease the crowded conditions of St. Philip's.

The act authorizing a new Anglican parish stipulated that St. Philip's Parish be split into two parishes, with Broad Street as the dividing line. The act directed that St. Michael's Church be erected on or near the place where the old wooden St. Philip's had stood, at a cost to the public of no more than £17,000. A new rector or minister was to be paid £150 per year and enjoy the same privileges as other ministers in the province.

A special pew was set apart for the governor and council and two large pews were designated for members of the Commons House of Assembly with another pew set aside for strangers. The remaining pews were to be of equal size, with those who contributed the most toward the building of the church to have first choice.

The architecture of St. Michael's was patterned after James Gibbs' St. Martin-in-the-Fields, London. The main body of the church is brick covered with stucco; the steeple and portico are wood. The freestanding Doric portico was similar to those of St. Philip's Church. Evidence indicates that St. Michael's original design included porticoes for the sides of the church, however, as costs mounted the side porticoes were eliminated. The first architect was a "Mr. Gibson," but Samuel Cardy, formerly of Dublin, completed the church.

Representation in the Assembly was equally divided between the two parishes. To prevent families from being separated, the inhabitants of either parish could bury their dead in the parish of the other. Nobody was permitted to have a pew in each church unless he owned a house in both parishes.

Nine commissioners were appointed to oversee the building of the church and parsonage and to receive subscriptions. On February 17, 1752, Governor James Glen laid the cornerstone in an auspicious ceremony that was followed by a grand dinner. Afterwards, His Majesty's health was drunk, followed by a salvo by the Granville Bastion cannon. Then the health of the royal family and other toasts were announced and drunk. According to the *Gazette,* the day was concluded with "peculiar pleasure and satisfaction."

Construction progressed rapidly at first, but by January 1754 the public treasurer had paid out £15,000. It was obvious that the church would cost far more than originally anticipated.

The commissioners had expected the sale of pews to raise the remaining funds. In spite of their diligence, with the costs escalating and no end in sight, construction did not progress much faster than had the second St. Philip's. In addition, with the possibility of Britain declaring war on France, there was justifiable concern about depleting the treasury. As a result, no new appropriations were made for St. Michael's until 1757. When the commissioners pointed out that the steeple could be used as a landmark to guide ships into the harbor, money intended for a beacon was finally allocated to the church.

The first service at St. Michael's was performed in February 1761. From the very beginning, the congregations of St. Michael's and St. Philip's enjoyed a harmonious relationship and functioned very effectively together.

Prominent individuals buried at St. Michael's include Charles Cotesworth Pinckney (1746-1825) and John Rutledge (1739-1800), signers of the U.S. Constitution; Brig. Gen. Mordecai Gist (1742-1792), Continental Army officer; Francis Kinloch (pronounced Kinlaw) (1755-1826) Continental Congress delegate; Robert Young Hayne (1791-1839) and Arthur Peronneau Hayne (c. 1789-1867), United States senators; William Dickinson Martin (1789-1833), U.S. congressman; and James Louis Petigru (1789-1863) Unionist.

Saga of the Bells

St. Michael's bells were purchased by public subscription and arrived from England in 1764. When the city was evacuated by the British in 1782, a British officer ordered the bells be removed from the steeple and taken to London. A London merchant who had formerly lived in Charles Town recognized the bells, bought them, and shipped them back. When they arrived the second time, citizens were overjoyed and hand-carried the bells from the wharf to the church and replaced them in the steeple.

The bells rang out every evening at curfew as well as on occasions of rejoicing and mourning. They called congregants to worship every Sunday until 1862 when they were sent to Columbia for safe keeping. In 1865, when Union Gen. William T. Sherman invaded South Carolina, he sent his army to Columbia instead of Charleston, and the bells were damaged in the conflagration that followed. In 1866, the damaged bells and fragments were sent to the successor of the London house that originally cast them. The metal was melted and recast with the same amalgam poured into molds made with the original trammels and again returned to Charleston. The city curfew was rung on the bells until September 4, 1882.

Anecdotes

St. Michael's steeple is topped with a sphere while St. Philip's had a weathervane in the shape of a rooster with a large tail. That prompted one wag to observe, "St. Michael's is the highball church and St. Philip's is the cocktail church."

In 1938, a tornado blew a hole in the roof of St. Michael's. An irreverent Charlestonian declared it an Act of God because, he said, "God had been trying to get into St. Michael's for 200 years."

The Middleton family attended St. Michael's because, as the family patriarch put it, "the Episcopal Church did not interfere with either your religion or your politics." This is supported by the story about a youngster who wanted to attend St. Michael's Sunday school. When the mother from another church told her child, "You go to a nice Sunday school," the child replied, "But Mother, you don't understand. At our Sunday school, all we hear about is God and Jesus and the Bible. At St. Michael's, it's different. They never talk about those things."

And there's the anecdote told of the Reverend William Percy. After the Revolution, three ministers were rotated between St. Michael's and St. Philip's churches. Rev. Percy's interminable evangelical sermons were delivered with broad motions and dramatic style. Worse, his wig covered his ears as he thumped the pulpit cushions, and he sometimes leaned over the desk to rap the head of the clerk at his desk below if the unfortunate showed signs of drowsiness or inattention. One day a "gentleman" at St. Michael's swore that he would pull him out of the pulpit if he attempted to preach. The man sneaked a cast net into the church and sat in front of the south gallery near the pulpit. All went well until Percy ascended the pulpit and began to speak. As the minister stepped down from the pulpit, the man heaved the net, which fortunately got hung up on the platform's sounding board. Although congregants managed to subdue the man, his shocking actions still make a good story.

More recently, two St. Michael's parishioners were the late Jane Lucas Thornhill and the late Elizabeth Jenkins (Liz) Young, both tour guides and preservationists. The story about the way they braved a bulldozer to save a historical building is legendary.

In early 1971 the College of Charleston campus was growing. To make way for the new library, the Wagener House at 6 Green Street (now called Green Way) was scheduled to be torn down on Friday morning, February 12. The planners, however, had not taken into consideration two feisty Charleston matrons who opposed the demolition.

The Wagener House, a ca. 1817 single house, had been moved in 1966 from its original site at 6 Green Street for the creation of the College Mall (now called Cougar Mall). It stood on the new site until 1971, when it was in the way of constructing the Robert Scott Small Library building. The college planned to move the house to Coming Street, until a house-mover estimated it would cost $30,000, and there was no guarantee is would survive. President Ted Stern decided it would be more practical to demolish the house. However, it was a favorite of preservationists because of its quaint appearance and Adamesque architectural features.

The day before the destruction was to take place, a reporter for *The News and Courier* contacted both ladies because they were on the College's President's Advisory Committee on Historic Preservation, to get their input on a story he was writing about the scheduled demolition. The ladies were surprised because their committee had not been consulted about it.

Early the following day, they rushed uptown to Green Street. Liz Young knew the bulldozer driver, Bunt Fiske, so she put her foot on the bulldozer while Jane Thornhill hurried over to Stern's office. Of course, the driver did not proceed when Mrs. Young told him that she would lie down in front of the bulldozer's path if need be. Jane Thornhill, though, did not fare so well because President Stern was in New Orleans at a Southern Association of Colleges conference, but when he returned, the Wagener House was moved to 8 Green Street instead.

Meeting Street 1861, A. Meyer, artist. Courtesy
Library of Congress.

Truth is...

"South of Broad" is not an historical designation. As popula-
tions shifted on peninsular Charleston in the 1940s and '50s,
property below Calhoun Street became more valuable. "South
of Broad" was probably invented by a clever realtor. Rowena
Wilson Tobias, (who lived on South Battery) writing ca. 1947,
called the high society notion of "south of Broad" a "fiction."
Charlestonians who grew up the 1920s and '30s called it "Below the Drain," referring to a partially subterranean canal that
runs from Colonial Lake to the Ashley River. Real estate agents
surely knew "Below the Drain" would not do the job.

The Beef Market

The Beef Market stood in the northeast corner of the public square, a position indicating the importance of beef to the early Carolina economy. The market was destroyed in the Great Fire of 1796 and replaced by the present building at 80 Broad Street, now City Hall.

Before cash crops like Carolina Gold rice became established, cattle raising was an important economic activity. The term "cowboy" was used in Carolina long before it was common to the West, designating a man or youth, frequently a slave, who rounded up the cattle. Cattle ranged freely in the woods, swamps, and grasslands of the Lowcountry. Free ranging was an African, not a European, tradition, and was one of many West African contributions to Lowcountry culture.

Beef was an important export. After butchering, the beef was salted and packed in barrels for shipment. A prime market was Barbados and other West Indian colonies, where the valuable sugar cultivation left little space for grazing cattle. In 1680 four tons of salt meat (beef and pork) were shipped to Barbados.

In 1692, Bernard Schinkingh had 292 cattle and three cowboys to herd them. James Joyner had 200 head, with three cowboys. Mounted cowboys kept track of the cattle and protected them from predators. They rounded them up for branding and for safety in cow pens.

Colonial herds numbered in the hundreds, and some owners had as many as a thousand. After arriving in 1671, Gov. John Yeamans sent to Virginia for 100 head of cows. In 1710 Thomas Nairne, in his *Letter from South Carolina*, said the province "abounds with black Cattle, to a Degree much beyond any other English colony."

With so many ranging loose, it was necessary to brand the cattle, and by law, no animal could be slaughtered unless its owner was known. The Livestock Mark Books are among the earliest surviving colonial records.

The Rutledge Brothers

John Rutledge and his brother Edward were "founding fathers" of the United States, Edward as a signer of the Declaration of Independence in 1776 and John as a drafter and signer of the United States Constitution in 1787.

They were sons of Dr. John Rutledge and Sarah Hext. Both attended the prestigious London law school, the Middle Temple. South Carolina had more students at London law schools than any other colony, reflecting the wealth of the province.

Both John and Edward served in the Commons House of Assembly, the First and Second Provincial Congresses and the General Assembly after the formation of state government in 1776.

John Rutledge (1739-1800). Courtesy Library of Congress.

In 1765, John was a delegate to the Stamp Act Congress in New York, where he helped write a petition to the House of Lords. He was elected president of the state in 1776 and was governor, from 1779 to 1782. He was known as "Dictator" Rutledge because of the extraordinary wartime powers granted to him.

John Rutledge was elected to the Congress of the Confederation in 1782. In 1789, he was appointed an associate justice of the U.S. Supreme Court by President George Washington. He resigned to become chief justice of the South Carolina Supreme Court in 1791.

Washington commissioned him chief justice of the U.S. Supreme Court in a recess appointment in 1795. However, the U.S. Senate, because of Rutledge's opposition to Jay's Treaty, which did not provide compensation for slaves confiscated by the British during the Revolution, did not confirm him. He died in 1800 and was buried in St. Michael's Churchyard.

Edward Rutledge (1749-1800) by Philip F. Wharton, after James Earl (Earle). Courtesy Independence National Historical Park.

Edward Rutledge formed a successful law practice with Charles Cotesworth Pinckney, who with John Rutledge was a signer of the Constitution.

After British Admiral Richard Howe won the Battle of Long Island in 1776, he asked the Continental Congress to negotiate peace. Congress sent Edward Rutledge, John Adams, and Benjamin Franklin, but the negotiations failed because Howe demanded immediate surrender of American troops.

In July 1776, Edward was twenty-six and the youngest of the signers of the Declaration of Independence.

John Rutledge House, 116 Broad Street. Tradition says he built it for his teenage bride, Elizabeth Grimké, in 1763. The house was remodeled to its present appearance in 1853 by Swedish architect P.H. Hammarskold. The ironwork was by Charleston artisan Christopher Werner. Courtesy Library of Congress.

In 1780 Edward was an artillery officer at the Siege of Charles Town. After the fall of the city, he was exiled to St. Augustine until he was exchanged in July 1781.

In 1794 President Washington offered Edward an appointment as associate justice on the U.S. Supreme Court, but he declined. Edward was a presidential elector in 1788, 1792, and 1796. He was elected governor in 1798. Tradition says Edward's fatal stroke in 1800 was caused by news of Washington's death. He was buried in St. Philip's Churchyard.

117 Broad Street was built ca. 1760 for James Laurens by carpenters Miller and Fullerton. In 1788, Edward Rutledge bought the house which was directly across the street from his brother John. Located on the north end of the Orange Garden, for which Orange Street was named, the house originally was Georgian Palladian in style. It was Victorianized by Capt. Frederick Wagener, whose family acquired it in 1885, and remodeled in Colonial Revival mode by Dr. Josiah Smith in 1935. Courtesy Library of Congress.

Shepheard's Tavern, as rebuilt after the Great Fire of 1796. Courtesy St. Philip's Church.

Shepheard's Tavern

Shepheard's Tavern (also known at various times as Swallow's Tavern, The City Tavern, and The Corner Tavern) was a site of many Charleston's "firsts."

In the early days of the colony, Charles Town had few public buildings, and its taverns served in a surrogate capacity. One stood out from all the rest: Shepheard's Tavern was strategically located midway between the State House at the corner of Broad and Meeting streets and The Exchange and Custom House at Broad and East Bay. It was patronized by the city's power brokers.

The original tavern fronted Broad Street and had a long room stretching along its Church Street side. For some years prior to 1738, this room was rented to the provincial government for court meetings. Thereafter, the long room was known as "the Courtroom."

The Courtroom was used for a variety of entertainments. Henry Holt, a dancing master, gave a ball there in December 1734. On January 11, 1735, The *South-Carolina Gazette* announced that Thomas Otway's tragedy, *The Orphan, or the Unhappy Marriage*, would be attempted in the Courtroom later that month. This was Charles Town's first record of a theatrical season. *The Orphan* was not the town's first theatrical production. In 1703, English actor Anthony Aston wrote and acted in his play, *The Country*, which was probably the first professional dramatic performance in the American colonies.

Shepheard's Tavern was a venue for banquets honoring the arrival of Royal governors. The site served as a post office in 1743 when Shepheard received and distributed the mail arriving by ship and by land. Solomon's Lodge No. 1, Free and Accepted Masons, was organized at "Mr. Charles Shepheard's in Broad Street" on Oct. 29, 1736. It was the second Masonic lodge in the English colonies, after the Boston lodge, established in 1733.

In 1773, when the establishment was known as Swallow's Tavern, the first city Chamber of Commerce in America was formed on the site. The St. Andrew's Society and other fraternal organizations held their meetings and dinners at Shepheard's. During the Revolutionary period, the tavern hosted meetings of the Sons of Liberty. On August 29, 1783, forty-three Continental officers assembled at the tavern and formed the South Carolina Society of the Cincinnati.

In 1796, the tavern burned but was soon replaced. In 1803, the first Scottish Rite lodge, the Supreme Council, 33rd Degree, Ancient and Accepted Scottish Rite of Free Masonry was founded there. Among its founders were some of Charleston's most accomplished citizens: Dr. James Moultrie, the only native South Carolinian among the original members; Dr. Isaac Auld, noted Charleston physician; and the Reverend Doctor Frederick Dalcho, author of *An Historical Account of the Protestant Episcopal Church in South Carolina*, the first diocesan history published in the United States. Moultrie went into practice with Dr. Isaac Auld and was elected to the Medical Society South Carolina. When he tried to resign from the Medical Society, they made him a lifelong honorary member.

Another distinguished Scottish Rite Freemason was Dr. Albert Gallatin Mackey, a graduate of the Medical College of South Carolina. In 1844 he abandoned the practice of medicine and devoted the rest of his life to writing and lecturing on a variety of arcane subjects. He was opposed to secession from the Union and was confined within Charleston's city limits during the war. His home was hit three times by shells from the Union bombardment. In July 1865, President Andrew Johnson appointed him collector of the port. Mackey was active in Republican politics during Reconstruction. In 1870 Mackey moved to Washington, D.C., and wrote numerous books about Freemasonry. Mackey enjoyed a national reputation for his keen wit, lively repartee, and remarkable anecdotal skills. He died in 1881 and was buried in Washington, D.C. His *Encyclopedia of Freemasonry* is still read and studied today.

The last tavern building on the site became a 19th century grocery store — Klinck and Wickenberg. The building was demolished in 1928 to make way for the construction of the Citizens and Southern Bank. Built in 1929, the Neoclassical bank was designed by Norwegian-born Savannah architect Otto Olaf.

Citizens and Southern Bank Building, 46 Broad Street. Photograph by Richard P. Donohoe.

A National Treasure

Nineteenth century view from East Bay looking north to the Exchange. The cupola was designed in 1833 by Charles Fraser to replace the original which was destroyed by storm. W. Gilmore Simms was critical of it, comparing it to a "pepper-box on a terrapin's back." Courtesy College of Charleston, Addlestone Library, Special Collections, Waddell Collection.

Charleston's Old Exchange and Custom House is one of the three most historic public buildings in the United States, along with Independence Hall in Philadelphia and Faneuil Hall in Boston. This prominence is well deserved, for colonial Charles Town was one of the busiest and richest ports on the Atlantic seaboard.

The foot of Broad Street had been occupied since early colonial days. A half-moon battery was built there before 1686. Beginning in 1704, a public building was on the site, with a Guard House and a Council Chamber above it where the governor met with the Grand Council, which was appointed by the Lords Proprietors.

By the 1760s maritime trade was so voluminous that Charles Town needed a building for both commercial and customs services. The city's wealthy merchants and investors petitioned the Assembly, which in 1767 granted £60,000 to build the Exchange

Half Moon Battery, with the Guard House/Council Chamber, detail from "An Exact Prospect of Charles-Town the Metropolis of the Province of South Carolina," by Bishop Roberts, 1739, engraved by William Henry Toms for *London Magazine*, 1762. Courtesy College of Charleston, Addlestone Library, Special Collections, Waddell Collection.

and Custom House on the site of the old Guard House/Council Chamber.

Original plans for a Palladian structure designed by William Rigby Naylor, an Irish architect, survive. The builders were German immigrant brothers John Adam and Peter Horlbeck. Expensive materials were imported: London crown glass windowpanes, Portland stone decorations, Purbeck stone paving and Carnarvon slate roofing. The basement contained fireproof storage cellars for rent and public use. Construction began in 1768 and was completed in 1771. Upon completion, it was the finest public building in British America.

The imposing new Exchange and Custom House dominated the harbor. Arriving dignitaries were greeted on its steps, and incoming merchantmen paid duties at the Custom House. It is said that as many as 300 vessels simultaneously occupied the harbor, everything from large sailing vessels to plantation barges and Indian canoes.

Significant History

In early July 1774, South Carolina citizens met in the Great Hall of the Exchange and elected delegates to the First Continental Congress. On March 28, 1776, a public reading of the state's constitution and the introduction of its president, John Rutledge and vice president, Henry Laurens, took place at the Exchange. On August 5, 1776, the Declaration of Independence was proclaimed publicly from both the State House balcony overlooking Meeting Street and the steps of the Exchange.

In 1780 a British force commanded by Sir Henry Clinton occupied the city. Clinton promised pardon of all "treasonable offences" if rebels swore loyalty to the Crown. Some Patriots refused to take the oath and were exiled to St. Augustine. Some were imprisoned in the Provost Dungeon beneath the Exchange. Some were paroled on their word that they would not take up arms against the Crown. And some unfortunates were placed in prison ships anchored in the harbor.

Patriot martyr Isaac Hayne was imprisoned in the Provost dungeon and spent his final days in a small room off the Exchange Great Hall.

The British occupied the Exchange for two and a half years and

The Exchange Building was wrecked by the 1886 Earthquake. Damage was so extensive that the federal government considered its demolition. Local sentiment, however, was for preserving the building. Courtesy The Charleston Museum.

never discovered 10,000 pounds of gunpowder that Gen. William Moultrie had stored behind a false brick wall.

The City of Charleston was incorporated in 1783, and the Exchange served as City Hall until 1818.

In 1818, the City of Charleston conveyed the Exchange building to the federal government. The building served as the Post Office, Custom House, and meeting hall. Slaves were sold on the north side of the building.

Thomas Bacot was a notable postmaster. His innovations included the first railroad shipment of mail. The Post Office moved in 1896 to the present building at Broad and Meeting.

In 1913, the Rebecca Motte Chapter of the Daughters of the American Revolution (DAR) acquired the Exchange and Custom House in trust as a historical monument.

The Ratification Convention

When the U.S. Constitutional Ratification Convention met at the Exchange in May, 1788, the issue of ratification was hotly contested. Charleston ws staunchly Federalist and favored ratification. Charleston and the Lowcountry parishes held a numerical majority. Most Backcountry delegates were Anti-Federalists. Influenced by Jeffersonian democratic ideals, they said the proposed Constitution was elitist and did not safeguard individual liberties.

There were eloquent speeches on both sides, but the Federalist majority prevailed. On May 23, 1788, South Carolina became the eighth state to ratify. Historian George C. Rogers Jr. observed: "Charleston was now at the peak of her importance. Without the city, the state would not have been for ratification. Without South Carolina, there would have been no United States."

William Pitt's Statue

To raise money to pay for colonial protection during the French and Indian War in 1765, Parliament required that printed materials in the colonies carry an embossed revenue stamp. This included legal documents, licenses, wills, diplomas, contracts, magazines, playing cards, newspapers, and many other types of paper used throughout the colonies. Only British coin was accepted as payment, not colonial currency.

View of St. Michael's and the State House with the statue of William Pitt at the intersection of Meeting and Broad streets, drawing by Charles Fraser, ca. 1800. Courtesy College of Charleston, Addlestone Library, Special Collections, Waddell Collection.

This act caused an outpouring of colonial opposition. Political leaders convened the Stamp Act Congress in New York, and South Carolina's Christopher Gadsden was a key player. While he was clamoring for legislative redress in New York, his constituency of local master artisans, known as the Mechanicks, continued agitating in Charles Town. They met under a live oak tree in Isaac Mazyck's pasture (at Alexander Street just north of present-day Calhoun Street).

Christopher Gadsden, portrait by Jeremiah Theus. Courtesy Library of Congress.

By the end of 1765 all colonial assemblies except those of Georgia and North Carolina had sent formal protests against the Stamp Act to England. Organized groups calling themselves the Sons of Liberty coalesced throughout the colonies, and riotous demonstrations along the eastern seaboard intimidated stamp-tax distributors into resigning their commissions.

Charles Town's duly-appointed royal inspector of stamp duties was George Saxby. He had emigrated from London in 1731 when the Crown appointed him searcher of the customs. He expanded his financial base through highly successful shipping and mercantile partnerships and a rice plantation near Georgetown. He also speculated in land, acquiring more than 6,000 acres of royal grants in Craven and Granville counties. Saxby advanced socially through his wife, Elizabeth Seabrook, who had inherited a 200-acre plantation on Johns Island and a brick house on Tradd Street in Charles Town.

Saxby's fortunes began to decline in 1765 when he visited England and received the appointment of stamp duties inspector. In Charles Town an angry mob ransacked his house, searching for the detested stamps, and burned him in effigy. Although Saxby suspended his duties as inspector when he returned to Carolina, the acrimony affected his mental and physical health. He developed signs of apoplexy and never fully recovered. In 1772 he and his wife sailed for England, never to return. During the Revolution, South Carolina authorities confiscated his property, leaving Saxby financially ruined. He died in penury in 1786.

The Statue

The Stamp Act was repealed March 18, 1766. When the news reached Charles Town, twenty-six members of the Sons of Liberty celebrated by meeting in Mazyck's pasture. After Christopher Gadsden addressed the group, the men joined hands around the oak tree and described themselves defenders and supporters of American Liberty. Thereafter, the place was known as the Liberty Tree.

William Pitt the Elder, first Earl of Chatham, British secretary of state and later prime minister, was largely responsible for the Stamp Act's repeal. The S.C. Commons House of Assembly commemorated the occasion by appropriating £7,000 for a marble statue to be carved by the celebrated English builder and sculptor Joseph Wilton.

Wilton depicted Pitt dressed in a toga with one arm holding the Magna Carta and the other extended upward. His masterpiece was escorted by an assistant and arrived on the *Carolina-Packet* at Charles Elliott's wharf on May 31, 1770.

Charles Town celebrated. Vessels in port were festooned, and St. Michael's Church stopped ringing its bells only because Isaac Mazyck was lying desperately ill nearby. Citizens "of the highest rank" hauled the statue up Broad Street to the Arsenal, then located across from the church. It remained there until master builders John and Peter Horlbeck erected a pedestal in the center of the intersection at Broad and Meeting streets.

As described in the *South-Carolina Gazette*, on July 5, 1770, the Honorable Peter Manigault officiated at the statue's installation. Afterwards, Pitt's health was toasted, and the artillery saluted Pitt. Gentlemen of Charles Town then retired to a tavern for speeches and forty-five ceremonial toasts, saluting everyone from the king and royal governor to such diverse miscellany as "all honest, resolute and disinterested patriots," "the virtuous minority of both Houses of Parliament," and "Judas' fate to the enemies of America."

The Statue's Odyssey

Enthusiasm for Wilton's marble masterpiece eventually waned. In 1780 British cannon fire struck off Pitt's extended left arm. By 1794 the disfigured statue in the center of the intersection was considered a nuisance, and City Council contracted for its removal. In the process, the head was broken off, and the statue's pieces were stowed in various public buildings. Judge John Faucheraud Grimké purchased the marble pedestal stones and placed the inscription slab in his garden at 321 East Bay Street.

In 1808 the Commissioners of the Orphan House got permission from City Council to erect the statue on their property. It remained there for nearly seventy-five years "surrounded by groups of happy children, impressively reminding them of the Great Charter of our Liberties, the symbol of which had been shattered when the arm that held it was carried away by the British cannon ball." This paean was slightly in error. The upraised left arm, removed by the British cannonball, had not held the Magna Carta. The charter had been in the statue's right arm, the hand and forearm of which were also missing by the time the statue was erected in the Orphan House yard.

The Pitt Statue at the Charleston Orphan House, right foreground. Courtesy Library of Congress.

Upon a request by the South Carolina Historical Society in 1881, the city moved Pitt's statue to the public area behind City Hall, then being redesigned as Washington Square. The new pedestal was red and buff brick on a base of Winnsboro granite. There were two marble inscription panels: the original, which Grimké had given to the Orphan House, and one commemorating the relocation.

A hundred years later, the statue was moved to the lobby of The Charleston Museum. In 2002, it was relocated again — this time to the loggia of the Charleston County Judicial Center located near the original site at the intersection of Broad and Meeting streets.

After the statue was removed, the brick pedestal stood empty in Washington Square for over a decade. In 1992, a committee headed by Gen. William Westmoreland raised funds and commissioned a bronze statue of George Washington by Charleston artist John Michel. Washington's monument was placed on the pedestal and dedicated in 1999.

The Pitt Statue in Washington Square. Courtesy Library of Congress.

Charles Town's Tea Party

In 1773 the Tea Act was passed in Parliament to rescue the financially beleaguered East India Company by giving it a monopoly to sell tea in the colonies. In September and October 1773, seven ships carrying East India Company tea set sail: four to Boston, and one each to New York, Philadelphia, and Charles Town.

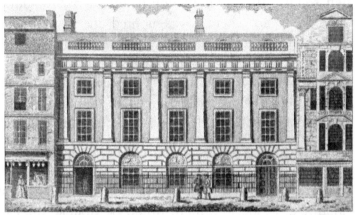

East India Company headquarters in London at the time of the Charles Town Tea Party. Engraving by T. Simpson, published in John Entick, *A New and Accurate History and Survey of London*, 1766.

The Sons of Liberty began a campaign to force consignees to resign, as had tax agents during the Stamp Act crisis. The New York and Philadelphia agents resigned under pressure, and the tea was returned to England. When three ships arrived in Boston on December 16, 1773, a group of men disguised as Mohawk Indians boarded the vessels and dumped 342 chests of tea into the water.

In November 1773 the *South-Carolina Gazette* editorialized that Parliament was determined "to raise a revenue, out of your pockets, against your consent — and to render assemblies of your representatives totally useless."

A few days later on December 1, under command of Capt. Alexander Curling, the *London* arrived with 257 chests of tea consigned to agents of the East India Company. A mass protest meeting was called, and on December 3 citizens from various socio-economic classes met in the Great Hall of the Exchange to discuss how to prevent the tea from being unloaded. They eventually adopted a non-importation resolution. Historians agree that this meeting laid the groundwork for an independent government in South Carolina.

When some radicals anonymously threatened to burn the *London* and the wharf where it was moored, the intimidated merchants agreed not to receive the tea. Because no one appeared to pay the duty on the cargo within the legal time limit, officials seized the tea and stored it in the Exchange. The tea remained there until the South Carolina government auctioned it, with the proceeds going into state coffers. Charles Town was the only port to permit tea to be brought ashore.

Charles Town had its own "Tea Party" on November 3, 1774, when the *Britannia* arrived from London carrying seven chests of East Indian tea. Suspecting there would be trouble, the captain of the ship, Samuel Ball, Jr., swore under oath before a notary in England that the Charles Town merchants who ordered the tea acted without his knowledge or consent. When the ship arrived, he "acknowledged having the mischievous Drug on Board," but was spared reprisals.

The consignees — merchants Robert Lindsay, Zephaniah Kingsley, and Robert Mackenzie fared less well. They were forced to board the *Brittania* and dump all seven chests of tea overboard. A crowd ashore gave three hearty cheers after the emptying of each chest. The *South-Carolina Gazette* later reportd, simply: An "Oblation was made to Neptune, of the said seven Chests of Tea."

Isaac Hayne and Mad Archie Campbell

Isaac Hayne was a respected member of the planter elite. Born in Colleton County in 1745, he inherited Hayne Hall in St. Bartholomew's Parish. He expanded his holdings to Sycamore and Pearhill plantations, land in the Backcountry and in Georgia, lots in Charles Town and Beaufort, and an interest in an ironworks in York District. Like many gentlemen of his era, he had a stable of thoroughbred horses.

He represented St. Bartholomew's Parish in the Commons House of Assembly from 1770 to 1771. Hayne was elected without his knowledge to the General Assembly, which adopted the Constitution of 1778, but he declined to serve. He later represented St. Bartholomew's Parish in the South Carolina Senate in 1779-80.

When the British invaded the state, Hayne raised a company of volunteer cavalry and was a captain in the Colleton County Regiment, although he later resigned after failing to be named colonel

Capture of Isaac Hayne and Death of McLaughlin. Lt. Col. Thomas McLaughlin, who served with Hayne in the Colleton County Regiment, was killed July 8, 1781 at the Horse Shoe, while Hayne was captured. Woodblock illustration from Horatio Newton Moore, *The Life and Times of Gen. Francis Marion* (Philadelphia: Leary, Getz, 1845). Courtesy Special Collections and Archives Division, Robert M. Strozier Library, Florida State University.

of the troop. Reenlisting as a private, he continued to serve until the fall of Charles Town in May 1780.

British Occupation

More than 5,000 men surrendered when Charles Town fell. The British imprisoned members of the Continental Army and granted parole to the militia and civilians. Hayne was paroled under the terms of the Articles of Capitulation and returned to Hayne Hall to sit out the war.

When British fortunes began to decline, Sir Henry Clinton issued a proclamation demanding that all paroled militia return to Charles Town and take an oath of allegiance to the Crown. Because of his popularity, Hayne was pressured to go to Charles Town by a colonel in the Loyalist militia. However, he was able to negotiate a written statement declaring that he would not "demean himself as a British subject so long as the country should be covered by the British army."

The status quo would have continued had smallpox not raged at his plantation, leaving Hayne's wife and several children near death. Hayne went to Charles Town for medications and was required to swear allegiance to the Crown before being permitted to return home. He took the oath only after he was assured by the deputy British commandant that he would not be required to bear arms against his former compatriots. But when the British were forced to retreat to the Charles Town area, Hayne and other parolees were summoned to join the Royal Army. Hayne considered this a violation of the negotiated agreement and a release from his obligations to the British.

He joined Col. William Harden's forces as a militia colonel at the Horse Shoe on the Ashepoo River and was given command of a regiment. Having committed himself to the cause, Hayne entered the field with vigor. In a daring raid near Charles Town, Hayne kidnapped Gen. Andrew Williamson, a Patriot who had joined the

Loyalists and was under British protection. This was no ordinary abduction. Williamson was seized in bed without being given time to put on his clothes and was taken to the Horse Shoe camp.

The British were mortified that Williamson had been snatched under their very noses. Fearing he would be hanged as a traitor, they dispatched ninety dragoons to rescue him. The British surprised the camp at Horse Shoe, killing fourteen and wounding others.

Hayne's Capture and Execution

Isaac Hayne was captured under unusual circumstances. He had separated from the returning raiding party and gone to a nearby plantation to rest. When British cavalry suddenly galloped up the avenue, he mounted a fine thoroughbred with the whimsical name of King Herod. Unfortunately, the animal had become too heavy during his master's confinement and gave out while approaching a fence. Instead of pressing him to leap, Hayne dismounted and took down the barrier.

Free of the obstruction, Hayne continued on, leaping a ditch. When the side caved in, his horse fell. A Loyalist officer, Capt. Archibald (Mad Archie) Campbell, captured Hayne before he had time to remount. Hayne was brought to Charles Town and imprisoned in the Exchange's provost dungeon.

Hayne was promised a trial, and had counsel prepared to justify his conduct by the laws of nations and the usages of war. However, to discourage other militiamen from joining the Patriot cause, Francis, Lord Rawdon, the British commander, decided to make an example of Hayne. He ordered a court of inquiry to determine his fate.

Ultimately, a proper trial was refused, and Hayne was ordered for execution. The judgment caused Lt. Gov. William Bull and town residents, both Loyalists and Patriots, to intercede. Ladies signed a petition on his behalf. His children, accompanied by their aunt and her daughter, begged Lord Rawdon for his life on bended knees in the great parlor of the Brewton Mansion on King Street, where the British commander was lodged. British commanders were inflexible.

Hayne was given a forty-eight-hour reprieve to say farewell to his children and spent his last days in the small room off the Great Hall of the Exchange. His final request was that he be permitted to die like a soldier, but even that request was denied without his knowledge.

He was taken from his cell and escorted by 300 men through thousands of anxious spectators to gallows just outside the city gate. When he saw that he would be hanged as a common criminal instead of being shot, his demeanor was described as heroic. After the execution, his thirteen-year-old son was permitted to bury his father's body at Hayne Hall.

Indignant at his captive's fate, Campbell declared that if he had known Hayne would be hanged, he would have killed him himself so he would have died the death of a soldier.

Aftermath

The hanging of Col. Isaac Hayne became a cause célèbre on both sides of the Atlantic. Rawdon's strategy may have discouraged more defectors in Carolina, but Yorktown fell on October 19, 1781. It was a humiliating defeat, when more than 7,000 men surrendered. Outraged at Hayne's execution, the South Carolina delegation to Congress made an unsuccessful motion to have the British general executed in retaliation for Hayne, but despite the calls for revenge, no British officer suffered Hayne's fate.

Capt. (Mad Archie) Campbell had a checkered career. His nickname had been given by brother officers who knew his violent temper and impulsive behavior. He flirted with daughters of Loyalists, including Margaret Philp, whom he abducted and married at gunpoint by the Loyalist rector of St. James, Goose Creek. "Mad

Archie" was killed near Brabant plantation at Videau's Bridge on January 2, 1782. Mrs. Campbell died about a week later. South Carolina author William Gilmore Simms included her story in his novel *Katherine Walton*.

In 1782 Charles, Duke of Richmond, a member of the House of Lords, and a sympathizer of the colonists, unsuccessfully attempted to censure Lord Rawdon for Hayne's inglorious death. That same year, the British evacuated Charles Town on December 14.

Isaac Hayne's death was not forgotten. Simms included a character modeled after Hayne in his 1835 novel *The Partisan*. On November 19, 1929, the state erected a monument at his final resting place near Jacksonboro. At the Old Exchange, the room off the Great Hall has been dedicated to his memory.

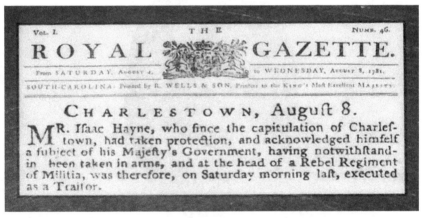

Royal Gazette, notice of Isaac Hayne's execution. Courtesy Library of Congress.

The Forgotten Signer

Pierce Butler, a signer of the United States Constitution in 1787, is a Founding Father with a colorful history. Born in 1744, he was the third son of Sir Richard Butler, fifth baronet of Clough-grenan in County Carlow, Ireland. As was the custom of the day, primogeniture prevented inheritance of his father's estate and the titles associated with it. To secure his future, a commission in the King's army was purchased when he was only eleven years old. By the time he was fourteen, he was fighting the French in North America. By 1762 he had served in Canada and had been posted to Boston to quell disturbances.

Pierce Butler, miniature attributed to Albert
Rosenthal. Courtesy National Archives.

Butler was twenty-two when he arrived in Carolina, already promoted to major "without purchase" in His Majesty's 29th Regiment. Smartly attired in his red uniform, he must have cut a dashing figure. He soon captured the affections of fifteen-year old Betsy Izard, an heiress with a considerable fortune. Betsy (Elizabeth) was a daughter of John Izard, brother of Ralph Izard. After a brief courtship, the aspiring groom made clandestine arrangements for an elopement. He borrowed a house in Goose Creek and hired a parson before his plans were discovered by Betsy's stepfather, who quickly spirited his young charge away.

Once freed of Butler's designs, Betsy wanted nothing more to do with him and later married Alexander Wright, son of the governor of Georgia, Sir James Wright. Alexander Wright was a Loyalist whose American estates were confiscated after the Revolution. However, his and Betsy's son, Sir James Alexander Wright, inherited his grandfather's baronetcy and English estates.

Butler returned to his regiment, and after an extended stay in England, he was back in Charles Town in early 1771 and promptly married another heiress, Mary Middleton, orphaned daughter of Thomas Middleton and Joanna Gibbes. He was then firmly established in Lowcountry society. When his regiment returned to England two years later, Butler resigned his army commission and stayed in Charles Town.

From then on, Butler devoted his time to advancing his social, political, and economic ambitions. The route to wealth was land, and he proceeded using the considerable social connections his marriage provided. His first acquisition was a sizeable estate his wife inherited from her grandmother Mary Branford Bull, including land on Bull's Island and Hilton Head Island. Butler also acquired 10,000-plus acres of grants that included 8,000 acres inland. He also formed a land speculation partnership that acquired 100,000 acres in Ninety-Six District. Using funds from the sale of his military commission, he purchased a 1,700-acre plantation on St. Simon's Island, and 1,800 acres of undeveloped land in Georgia. In addition, he acquired 10,000 acres in Tennessee and property in Philadelphia. By 1800 he owned six large rice and cotton plantations in Georgia and 540 enslaved workers.

During the Revolution, Butler sided with the colonials, initially as an adviser. In 1779 Governor John Rutledge appointed him adjutant general and later a brigadier general. Butler helped organize, train and mobilize the S.C. militia. But Butler preferred the rank of major, which was his highest combat role. He was present at the attack on Savannah as aide-de-camp to Gen. Lachlan McIntosh, and commanded raids on Gen. Augustine Prévost's forces in the Lowcountry. A former Royal officer, he was a target for capture, barely escaping on several occasions.

When the British occupied Charles Town in 1780, Butler was working with the partisan resistance forces of Francis Marion and Thomas Sumter, retreating later to North Carolina to work with Gen. Horatio Gates.

Butler paid a heavy price for his patriotism. He contributed some of his personal wealth at the end of the Southern Campaign, even while one of his plantations was burned and 200 of his slaves were confiscated. Worse, his family was exiled from Charles Town.

The war bankrupted Butler's business interests to the extent that he was forced to travel to Amsterdam to secure a loan. In 1784 he sailed to London with his son Thomas, and after enrolling him in a private school and obtaining a minister for St. Michael's Church, he traveled to the continent to borrow money, returning to South Carolina in the fall of the following year.

A practically illegible plaque on the west wall of St. Michael's vestibule documents his affiliation with the church. His wife, Mary Middleton Butler, was buried in St. Michael's Churchyard.

Political Influence

Partly to protect his interests, Butler got involved in politics, and after the Revolution served in the General Assembly. Originally, he espoused Federalist policies, but became a Jeffersonian in 1795 in opposition to Jay's Treaty and Federalist tariff measures. He advocated reconciliation with former Loyalists, equal representation for residents of the Upcountry, and he opposed printing paper money.

In 1787, Butler was one of four South Carolina delegates to the U.S. Constitutional Convention in Philadelphia. He introduced the Fugitive Slave Clause, a federal guarantee that runaways would be captured and returned to slaveholders, protecting their property rights. He supported counting all slaves for the purpose of Congressional representation, against Northern demands that slaves, as property, should not be counted for that purpose. The Three-Fifths Compromise, sponsored by South Carolina's Charles Pinckney, counted three-fifths of the slaves. This gave Southern states more Congressional representation, and power, than if the slave population had not been counted.

The richest South Carolina delegate, Butler attended the convention wearing a jacket trimmed with gold lace. Northern delegates referred to the South Carolinians as "nabobs" and "bashaws" (pashas) because of their wealth and bearing.

Butler was elected to the U.S. Senate in 1789. He held other national offices, including being a director of the Second Bank of the United States. He was described as arrogant, opinionated, and short tempered.

His political fortunes began to fade after he gave refuge to Aaron Burr, following the infamous duel with Alexander Hamilton. Both New York and New Jersey had indicted Burr for murder. To escape prosecution Burr traveled to Butler's St. Simons plantation under the name of Butler's overseer, Roswell King.

Pierce Butler spent his last years in Philadelphia where he died in 1822. He was buried in the Christ Episcopal Churchyard. Estranged from his son, his Mease grandchildren inherited his property and lost what remained after slavery was abolished.

Monsieur Placide's Affaires d'Amour

In 1792 Thomas Wade West and John Bignall, managers of the Virginia Company of Comedians, announced plans for a theatre in Charleston to be built on Savage's Green, a small piece of land between two tidal creeks at the west end of Broad Street. The theatre was designed by James Hoban, architect of the White House in Washington. The façade fronted Broad Street with a pit entrance located on what was then called Middleton Street. After the theatre was erected at the corner, Middleton Street became known as the New Theatre Street. Today, it is known as New Street.

The Broad Street Theatre, built in 1793, became the Medical College of the State of South Carolina in 1832. Courtesy Waring Historical Library, Medical University of South Carolina.

An announcement in the September 1792 issue of *New York Magazine* described the theatre as similar to the London Opera House. The façade featured a pediment, stone ornaments, a large flight of stone steps, and a courtyard. The article commented on the stage, the lighting, ceiling ventilation, and three tiers of box seats equipped with a window and venetian blind. It seated 1,200. The playhouse was built under West's direction.

At the time, West had nearly thirty years' experience in many of the major theatres of England, and he brought with him some English actors. The most famous were Matthew Sully and his talented family. Thomas, the fourth child, served as an acrobat on the stage when the family arrived in Charleston. He studied art, and later joined his older brother Lawrence Sully, a miniature painter, in Richmond. By 1809 Thomas Sully was in England receiving instruction from Benjamin West and Sir Thomas Lawrence. After the deaths of Charles Wilson Peale and Gilbert Stuart, Sully became the leading portrait painter in the United States.

The playhouse opened in 1793 during Race Week, the premiere event of Charleston's winter social season, when the elite were pampered with horse racing, balls, and entertainments. Performances included comic opera and dramatic productions ranging from Shakespeare to the latest offerings in New York and London's Covent Garden. The theatre was packed.

But the theatre closed when attendance fell off sharply during a recession in the early 1830s. It was purchased by the faculty of the Medical College of the State of South Carolina and became a teaching hospital, which was eventually supplanted by Roper Hospital on Queen Street. Hoban's historic building was torn down in 1850.

After the revolution in the French island colony of Saint-Domingue, Charleston welcomed many refugees. It was not long before French actors began performing at the Broad Street Theatre. But when John Bignall died in August 1793, trouble loomed.

In April 1794 a French theatre opened at Sollée's Hall, located on the west side of Church Street between St. Michael's Alley and Tradd Street. Comedians, pantomimists, and rope-dances inaugurated the French Theatre in a benefit performance, raising ransom money to free American prisoners held by Barbary pirates in Algiers.

Competition between the two theatres grew fierce. On Mondays, Wednesdays, and Fridays, Charleston's elite patronized Shakespearian and erudite performances on Broad Street, while extravagant French comedies, acrobatics and light opera were performed at Sollée's Hall on Tuesdays, Thursdays, and Saturdays.

The 1795 season in Charleston was considered the most brilliant musical year that had yet appeared in America. But the Broad Street theatre's popularity was waning, and by 1798 most of Thomas Wade West's performers had gone over to the French Theatre.

George Washington's death in December 1799 brought the city to mourning and served to unite the competing theatrical groups. After 1800 the Broad Street Theatre became Charleston's only playhouse, and was generally referred to as The Theatre.

Alexandre Placide

A performer of pantomimes, ballets and acrobatics, Alexandre Placide arrived in Charleston to manage John Sollée's French Theatre. He performed with the French troupe at the Broad Street theatre in the 1794-95 season, accompanied by his (maybe) wife, a beautiful ballerina named Suzanne Vaillande.

But apparently Mme. Placide had a wandering eye and eloped for parts unknown with Louis Douvillier, an actor from Paris. When Placide learned that Douvillier had returned to Charleston, he wrote him a note saying that if he did not leave immediately, one of them would die. Douvillier was so incensed that he promptly purchased two French rapiers, had their points sharpened and went in search of Placide.

Douvillier found Placide as he was leaving the theatre on Broad Street with a lady on his arm. Douvillier presented the hilts of the swords, telling Placide to make his choice and defend himself. As a chronicler told it, Placide did so "and like a flash of lightning at it they went, in the most public street of Charleston. The lady screamed and fainted; the passersby at once interfered, and the two were separated. Placide received a stab in the side, but not fatal. Two days after, Douvillier and Suzanne were not to be found." The couple headed for Virginia and re-engaged with Thomas Wade West, and within a few years they had settled in New Orleans, where Suzanne became the prima ballerina of the city.

Placide did not mourn the loss of his wife (or alleged wife), for long. In 1796 he married Charlotte Sophia Wrighten at the French Protestant (Huguenot) Church in Charleston. The minister was

Alexandre Placide, dancer, acrobat and theater manager.
Courtesy Harvard Theatre Collection, Houghton Library
Harvard University.

John Paul Costa, whose play, *America Preserved*, had been produced by Placide. The groom was forty-six, the bride about twenty.

Her mother was so shocked at the sudden marriage of her daughter to an already married man that it completely prostrated her. She was unable to recover and died of a broken heart twelve days later. Her funeral notice appeared in the *Gazette* on August 13, 1796. The disconsolate bride, bereft of her mother, pined away shortly thereafter.

Placide was manager of the theatre in Charleston from 1799 until his death in 1812. He was the most successful theater manager in the city's history, and by the end of his tenure, Charleston had emerged as one of four major theater centers in America.

The Two Capitals of South Carolina

Charleston had been politically dominant in South Carolina from its founding, but as the Backcountry grew in population, there arose a demand for a more centrally located state capital. Charlestonians were reluctant to give up their status, so their political leaders negotiated a compromise — the State Constitution of 1790. This remarkable document essentially gave South Carolina two capitals — one in Columbia and one in Charleston.

The 1790 Constitution required that the General Assembly meet in Columbia every November. The site of Columbia, on the Congaree River, had been chosen for the capital in 1786. As the legislature was the most powerful branch of state government, that satisfied residents of the Backcountry. But concessions were made to politically powerful Charleston.

The Charleston State House, officially known as the Charleston District Court House. Courtesy College of Charleston, Addlestone Library, Special Collections, Waddell Collection.

The constitution, which remained in place until 1865, required the governor to live in Columbia only during sessions of the General Assembly. At other times, the governor could reside "wherever in his opinion, the public good may require." There was no provision for a governor's mansion, so it was wherever the chief executive lived. When Edward Rutledge was governor in 1798-1800, and John Geddes in 1818-1820, their residences in Broad Street served as the governor's mansion.

Other executive offices were divided between the two cities. There were two treasurers, one in Charleston for Lower South Carolina and one in Columbia for Upper South Carolina. The secretary of state and the surveyor general maintained offices in both cities; each could choose to reside in either city, with a deputy to reside in the other.

The judiciary branch's highest court, the South Carolina Court of Appeals, held sessions in both cities, meeting first in Columbia and then in Charleston. In Charleston, the state judges met in the State House, which also housed the U.S. District Court until 1837.

State offices for Lower South Carolina were in the Charleston State House until 1826, when they moved to the newly completed Fireproof Building on Meeting Street just off Broad. They remained there until 1865, when a new constitution did away with the dual offices.

The Charleston State House

The colonial State House in Charles Town was part of a grand program of architectural embellishment for the provincial capital. Legislation adopted in 1751 called for building the State House, St. Michael's Church, and the Guard House all in the public square at Broad and Meeting streets. The State House and the church were expensively built in the prevailing Palladian high style, and probably the Guard House was as well.

The ambitious program reflected the wealth of the province, and the aspirations of its leaders to achieve their vision of a British colonial capital and port city. Charles Town was in many ways a "little London," as historian Robert Rosen noted.

State House in Columbia, *Harper's Weekly*, April 8, 1865. Illustration by William Waud.

The colonial State House burned in 1788, and the building was rebuilt in the same Palladian mode. Legislation authorizing the rebuilding called it the Charleston District Court House, but Charlestonians continued to call it the State House, with justification since it contained state offices. The basement and burnt-out walls of the colonial structure were incorporated into the new one. The new building looked very much like its predecessor, except for the addition of another story.

The state mace, not lost in the 1788 fire, today resides in the Senate chamber in Columbia, where it is carried in processions, as it was in the 18th century. Made in London in 1756 by Magdalen Feline, it is gilded silver and features a crown and the Hanover coat of arms.

Truth is...

The architect of the colonial State House in Charleston is unknown. Documentation points to Judge William Drayton, chairman of the building commission, as the designer of the replacement building, completed ca. 1790. There is no evidence it was designed by James Hoban, the architect of the White House, as some have alleged.

Designed by Robert Mills in the Rational Neoclassical style, the Fireproof Building was constructed in 1822-27 as a repository for Lower South Carolina state records. Courtesy Library of Congress.

House of National "Firsts"

At the northwest corner of Broad and King Streets is a wooden double house that is said to be the oldest frame structure in the city. It has had a series of very interesting owners.

The site, designated Lot 160 on the Grand Modell, was granted March 23, 1694 to James DeBordeaux, a Huguenot who arrived in Carolina with some of his wealth intact. DeBordeaux added to his holdings, acquiring the entire west side of King Street between what is now Broad and Queen streets. Before his death in 1699, he also had acquired two tracts totaling 500 acres in Berkeley County near St. Denis' Church.

Lining House, 106 Broad Street, when it had an apothecary in one corner. The Preservation Society of Charleston bought the house in 1961 and restored it. The apothecary shop is now in The Charleston Museum. Courtesy Library of Congress.

Chief Justice Hill

The wooden house at 106 Broad Street was first mentioned in a 1715 deed where William Livingston and his wife conveyed to William Harvey Jr., a butcher, the corner lot with "the messuage or tenem't thereupon standing." The deed indicates that the building had been rented to David Balentine before he died and was more lately rented to Mr. Harvey.

In 1728 Harvey and his wife sold the property to Charles and Elizabeth Hill. Charles Hill was a landowner and a merchant involved with the Indian trade. In 1715 he married Elizabeth Godfrey, daughter of Capt. John Godfrey, one of the original Barbadian settlers.

Using his wife's inheritance as a nucleus, Hill accumulated 300 acres, which he settled as Hillsboro plantation on Old Town Creek, a tributary of the Ashley River. Hill held many offices, among them chief justice of the Court of Common Pleas. He signed a petition asking for royal government to replace the Lords Proprietors, leading to the Revolution of 1719. Hill died in 1734 and left the Broad Street house to his wife. She later married the Reverend Samuel Quincy and bequeathed the property to her daughter Sarah, who had married Dr. John Lining.

John Lining — Pioneering Scientist, Meteorologist

John Lining (pronounced Linning) was born in Lanarkshire, Scotland, and immigrated to South Carolina about 1728. In 1733 he advertised various medicinal waters for sale at his shop on Broad Street "opposite Mr. Crokatt's" and later moved to another undocumented Broad Street location. Lining also owned two tenements on East Bay Street.

He joined the St. Andrew's Society, became physician to the poor of St. Philip's Parish, justice to the Court of General Sessions and the Court of Common Pleas, senior warden of Solomon's Lodge of Masons, and president of the Charles Town Library Society in 1750.

In 1737 Lining began the first systematic weather observations on the American continent made with scientific instruments. He also conducted experiments in human metabolism on himself and wrote the Royal Society of London that he had embarked on the observations to discover the influences of different seasons upon the human body. He corresponded about electricity with Benjamin Franklin in Philadelphia and carried out Franklin's kite and key experiment in a local thunderstorm.

Lining studied yellow fever and published one of the first accounts of that dreaded disease in North America. Believing that yellow fever was an imported disease, the General Assembly made more stringent quarantine regulations in 1737, and he was one of the three physicians mentioned in the act. Lining's experiments were published in the *Transactions of the Royal Society of London* and in *Gentlemen's Magazine*.

At the age of forty-six, Lining developed gout and was obliged to give up medical work. He spent his last years at Hillsboro plantation, where he experimented with electricity and indigo cultivation. Lining died in September 1760.

Attorney John Rattray

In 1751 the Reverend Mr. Quincy gave the Linings a quit claim to 106 Broad Street. That same day, the Linings conveyed the property to John Rattray, a prominent attorney and landowner.

The house was only steps away from the State House, the center of government, and Rattray used the building for his law office. He was appointed notary public by Governor James Glen, but lost the position when a Royal appointee [called a "placeman"] arrived two years later. Rattray served four terms in the Assembly and held numerous offices. In 1760 he was appointed judge of the Vice Admiralty Court, a position he held until his death the following year.

First Female Newspaper Publisher in America

Elizabeth Timothy (Timothee), publisher of the *South-Carolina Gazette*, purchased 106 Broad Street in 1786. John Whitemarsh, a protégé of Benjamin Franklin, had founded the *Gazette* in 1731. He was replaced three years later by another Franklin protégé, Lewis Timothy (Timothee).

When Lewis Timothy died in 1738, his widow, Elizabeth, and son, Peter, continued the paper, making Elizabeth the first woman editor and publisher in America. Their printing office had been located on the west side of King Street, just below Broad. Peter Timothy and his wife Ann later made the *South-Carolina Gazette* a major Patriot paper, and its publication was suspended during the British Occupation. When the British left in 1783, widowed Ann Timothy revived the paper as the *Gazette of the State of South Carolina*. After her death, the newspaper was continued until 1802 by her son Benjamin Franklin Timothy. During Timothy's ownership, the *Gazette* was published at 106 Broad Street.

Turnbull's Apothecary Shop

Dr. Andrew Turnbull arrived in Charles Town in 1781 and occupied 106 Broad Street. Turnbull was a Scots physician who served as British consul at Smyrna, a Greek city in the Ottoman Empire (now Turkey). He was a friend of James Grant, the governor of British East Florida, and secured a royal grant of 40,000 acres south of St. Augustine as the site of New Smyrna.

Turnbull returned to Europe and, in spite of local opposition, enlisted about 1,225 Minorcan and Greek colonists. Turnbull's settlers eventually grew crops of indigo, hemp, and sugarcane, but the plantation suffered major losses due to insect-borne diseases and Indian raids.

Tensions grew between Turnbull and the colonists because of his neglect and mistreatment by his overseers. In 1777, the colonists marched to St. Augustine, complained to the governor, and abandoned New Smyrna when he offered them sanctuary.

In 1781, when Spanish forces led by Bernardo de Gálvez captured British West Florida and their troop ships were advancing eastward to the Bahamas and East Florida, Turnbull left his plantation for Charles Town. His wife, Maria Gracia Dura Bin Turnbull, a native of Smyrna, is believed to have been the city's first Greek resident. Although he refused to renounce his loyalty to the Crown, Turnbull remained in South Carolina after the British evacuated Charles Town on December 14, 1782.

When Dr. Alexander Garden evacuated with the British, Turnbull acquired his large practice. His apothecary shop became very popular, so much so that Dr. David Ramsay wrote Dr. Benjamin Rush that "he had nearly as much practice as any three of his profession." Turnbull was one of the founders of the Medical Society of South Carolina and died in Charleston in 1792.

Turnbull's apothecary shop was the first of a series of drug stores in the building. At some point, the eastern half of the double-house was converted into a shop on the ground floor, and the east chimney was removed. In 1960 Schwettman's, the last establishment, closed and the apothecary shop interior was moved to The Charleston Museum.

In 1938 the City of Charleston erected a marker commemorating Dr. John Lining's connection to 106 Broad Street, and it has been called the "John Lining House" ever since. When this historical gem was threatened with demolition in 1961, the Preservation Society of Charleston bought the building and restored it. In 1972, it was sold as a private residence and is currently occupied by a law firm, which has taken great pride in their historic office building and done significant restorations inside and in the garden area.

America's Oldest Museum

The Charleston Museum was founded in 1773 by the Charles Town Library Society as a scientific and natural history museum. The Library Society had been established in 1748 by young men educated in London who wished to keep up with affairs in the imperial capital. In 1755, librarian William Henderson moved the library to his school on Broad Street. Natural history was a major interest of Society members, so in 1773 they began to collect scientific treatises, instruments, and specimens. Many of the original collections were destroyed by fire in 1778 and operations were suspended during the American Revolution. Collecting resumed in the 1790s, when the Library Society and its museum were in the upper floor of the State House. In 1824 the museum opened to the public.

The Charleston Museum photographed in 1932. The building was built in 1899 as Thomson Auditorium. The Charleston Museum acquired it in 1907. Courtesy The Charleston Museum.

The Library Society acquired the former bank building at 50 Broad Street in 1835 and maintained its library there until 1914, when it moved to its new building at 164 King Street.

In the meantime, the museum collections were brought to the College of Charleston in 1850. By 1852 Harvard scientist Louis Agassiz declared the museum to be among the finest in America. Operations were suspended during the Civil War. The museum was reorganized and transferred several times before it was established in the Thomson Auditorium.

Thomson Auditorium in Cannon Park on the west side of the Charleston peninsula had been completed in just ninety days for the United Confederate Veterans' Reunion held in May 1899. The reunion attracted 30,000 people. They were entertained with activities including a reenactment of the attack on Fort Sumter. The auditorium continued to serve as a convention meeting place until The Charleston Museum took it over in 1907. Renovation of the auditorium proceeded slowly, and it was ready for occupancy by the museum in 1909.

That year, the museum director, Dr. Paul Rea, hired Laura Bragg to be the curator of books and public instruction. One of Bragg's first duties was to relocate the museum collection from the College of Charleston to Thomson Auditorium. She set up exhibits using the artifacts that had been in storage and quickly transformed the museum into a public educational institution. Her innovations attracted thousands of new visitors. She also began lectures and established a reading room. Bragg founded the Charleston Free Library in 1930 as Charleston's first public library. Bragg also created the nation's first traveling exhibits for schools, which ultimately became a nationally recognized educational tool.

In 1915 the museum gained separate status from the college and was incorporated with a board of trustees. After Dr. Rea resigned in 1920, Bragg was named director upon his recommendation, as the first woman chosen to lead a major American museum. In that capacity, she worked for progressive social reform by crossing many social boundaries. In 1921 she opened The Charleston Museum to African Americans, four years after the trustees had formally restricted their admittance to Saturday afternoons. During her twenty-year tenure, museum attendance increased over 500 percent.

In 1931 Bragg took a five-year leave of absence to become the director of the Berkshire Museum in Pittsfield, Massachusetts, with the understanding that she would return to her old position. While she was gone, E. Milby Burton became head of the museum. Bragg returned to Charleston in 1939 to find that Burton would remain director.

In 1980 the museum moved to a new building on the northeast corner of Meeting and John streets. A fire destroyed Thomson Auditorium in October 1981, and only the front steps and four columns of the structure remain as a reminder of the museum's past.

Thomson Auditorium ruins. The building mysteriously burned in 1981, leaving only the portico base and columns. Photograph by Richard P. Donohoe.

The Legacy House

Many of the town lots along Broad Street were acquired by prominent settlers. One of them was Isaac Mazyck, a French Protestant (Huguenot) who left France during the religious persecutions of the late 17th century. Unlike most French Protestant immigrants, the Mazycks were Walloons of Liège, who moved to France for economic reasons when the government changed hands in their homeland.

Isaac Mazyck (1661–1735/36), miniature portrait by unknown artist. Courtesy Gibbes Museum of Art/Carolina Art Association.

Isaac Mazyck (pronounced Ma-ZEEK) was born in 1661 at St. Martin de Ré. His father had prospered in France and planned to establish his son in the business community. Unfortunately, this was at the time when Louis XIV turned up the campaign to eliminate Protestants, whom he regarded as heretics. In 1685, in a final attempt to force Protestants to convert to Catholicism, Louis XIV revoked the Edict of Nantes, a document that had protected their civil rights. After that, many Huguenots fled, fearing for their lives.

Isaac escaped with £1,000 sterling, a fortune in those days. He arrived in Charles Town in 1686 and acquired as much land as he could. In addition to being one of the largest land owners in South Carolina, Mazyck was also a merchant and highly successful business partner of Jacques Le Serrurier, a Huguenot from Picardy.

In 1693 Isaac married Le Serrurier's daughter Marianne. Mazyck died in 1735 and was buried at the east end of the Huguenot Church. In 1845, the present church was built over his grave, and his memory is perpetuated on a large marble tablet on the south wall of the church. Today the Mazyck name is associated primarily with the Mazyckborough neighborhood of Charleston and the pasture where Christopher Gadsden read the Declaration of Independence under a live oak, known as The Liberty Tree, which was destroyed by the British in 1780.

The Ravenels of Wantoot

Another reminder of Isaac Mazyck is the handsome brick single house at 68 Broad Street. Isaac Mazyck acquired the lot in 1710 from Gov. Robert Johnson. According to Ravenel family records, his granddaughter, Charlotte Mazyck, married Daniel Ravenel of Wantoot plantation. His son, another Daniel Ravenel, built the house on Broad Street.

The Ravenels originated in Brittany and arrived in Charles Town with other Huguenots in 1686. René Ravenel, the immigrant, secured 200 acres on the Santee River at Dutarte Creek. In 1697 he married the beautiful Charlotte de St. Julien at Pompion Hill, the newly settled plantation of Pierre de St Julien de Malacare. Family tradition is that René came to Carolina because he was smitten with Charlotte and had followed her from France.

A marriage certificate written in Latin memorialized the event. The certificate was a gift of Florent Trouillard, who officiated at the wedding. This document places René Ravenel and the father of the bride, Pierre de St Julien de Malacare, in the French Quarter on the East Branch of the Cooper River a year before extensive land grants lured them up the Santee River to St. John's, Berkeley, Parish. One of the Ravenel plantations there was Wantoot, which remained in the Ravenel family for generations.

68 Broad Street

Back in Charleston, the wooden house built on Isaac Mazyck's Broad Street lot burned in the Great Fire of 1796, and Daniel Ravenel II of Wantoot replaced it with the present-day house. The property included a kitchen house, a washhouse, a stable, and slave quarters. The property is now separated from Washington Square by a tall brick wall that was built when part of the original lot was taken for a public square.

Daniel Ravenel House. Built in 1796, it is a typical Charleston single house. Courtesy Library of Congress.

Before the Revolution, 68 Broad Street was prime real estate. The State House was only fifty paces from the Ravenel property. The house next door was rented by Lt. Gov. William Bull, and Justice William Burrows lived across the street.

68 Broad Street survived Union bombardment during the siege of Charleston, in spite of the fact that St. Michael's steeple across the street was a target for Union guns. It also survived the Earthquake of 1886. Hundreds of quake victims camped next door in Washington Park, and the property was used to assist with the feeding and caring for homeless refugees. In the 20th century, some damage occurred during a 1939 tornado that ripped off the roof of St. Michael's. Almost identical damage occurred during Hurricane Hugo in 1989.

The Ravenel home is the only legacy property that has been continuously owned by the same family. All owners were named Daniel Ravenel, except for one Henry. The current resident is the owner of one of Charleston's prominent real estate firms, unsurprisingly named Daniel Ravenel Real Estate Company, which is also on Broad Street.

"Let's Play Jazz on the Piazza"

The Charleston single house is not a style. It is a house type (or form) that adapted to changes in style. Thus, there are single houses in styles ranging chronologically from the Colonial Georgian to the Colonial Revival. A distinctive element is the piazza.

Architect Inigo Jones, in designing Covent Garden in the 1630s, was inspired by the Italian piazza, an open square with buildings around it, and a running arcade on their first level. He called the open square Covent Garden Piazza. But the English public, unfamiliar with the foreign term, began calling the arcades around the square, "piazzas." They also Anglicized the word. Thus, in English since the 1630s, a covered walkway has been called a piazza, pronounced to rhyme with "jazz." The earliest documented piazzas in the Lowcountry are those at Middleburg plantation house, built ca. 1697-99.

Hebrew Orphan Society

O n the corner of Broad Street and Court House Square is an imposing three-story building once owned by the Hebrew Orphan Society. The site originally belonged to Thomas Archdale, son of John Archdale, governor and lord proprietor.

Archdale Square encompassed much of the land bounded by Broad, King, Queen, and Meeting streets. When it was subdivided, the parcel for 88 Broad Street became Lot No. 315. Little development occurred on Archdale Square in the early years, possibly because it was outside the city wall. Lot No. 315 is thought to have been part of the site of Johnson's Ravelin fortification system when it was constructed in 1704.

Hebrew Orphan Society, 88 Broad Street. Courtesy Library of Congress.

John Laurens acquired Lot No. 315 in 1731 and built a rental property called White Hall. John's son, Henry, inherited White Hall and had the building demolished in 1771.

This was the same Henry Laurens who was president of the Continental Congress (1777-1778). He was captured by the British while en route to the Netherlands to negotiate a treaty, and was imprisoned for high treason in the Tower of London until his friends posted a bond for £10,000 sterling. Laurens was later exchanged for Lord Cornwallis, the British general who surrendered at Yorktown.

In March 1785, Henry Laurens advertised to sell Lot No. 315 "on which two small wooden houses now stand, but are to be removed." Henry Laurens died in 1792, and his oldest son, also Henry, inherited the property. In 1804 the lot was sold to attorney Edward Trescot for $12,000. In 1811 Trescot gave the property to his son, William, also an attorney. William Trescot served in the state militia as an ensign in an artillery company during the War of 1812 and served in the South Carolina General Assembly from 1814 to 1817.

The construction of 88 Broad Street is attributed to William Trescot. His estate sold 88 Broad Street to Theodore Hunt Thomas, and in 1833 the Hebrew Orphan Society purchased it from René Godard.

The acquisition of such a significant property signaled that the Hebrew Orphan Society was an integral part of the Charleston community, for at that time there were more benevolent societies in Charleston than anywhere else in the United States. The society placed a marble marker in both Hebrew and English on the building's façade proclaiming its founding in 1801. The Hebrew Orphan Society, along with other charitable organizations, gave balls to raise funds for the poor.

Jews were attracted to Carolina by religious freedoms granted in the Fundamental Constitutions. In 1695 Governor Archdale had a Jewish interpreter help in dealing with the Spanish.

By 1749, Kahal Kadosh Beth Elohim congregation was established. Jewish South Carolinians supported the Patriot cause in the American Revolution, notably Francis Salvador, who in 1775 became the first Jew elected to public office, serving in the First and Second Provincial Congresses.

The Hebrew Benevolent Society was founded in 1784 and is the oldest Jewish charitable society in the United States still in operation. In 1794 Jewish congregants built a handsome synagogue on Hasell Street, and by 1800, Charleston had the largest Jewish population in North America.

Members of the society participated in the elaborate funeral procession of John C. Calhoun in 1850, and when South Carolina seceded from the Union, many Jewish Charlestonians donned Confederate uniforms.

The first Synagogue Beth Elohim on Hasell Street. Built in 1794, it burned in the Great Fire of 1838. Courtesy College of Charleston, Addlestone Library, Special Collections, Waddell Collection.

The Hebrew Orphan Society used 88 Broad Street for meetings and educational purposes. It did not house orphans except for a brief time before the Civil War. Instead, society members placed orphans in private homes, donated clothes, and provided education and money for their upkeep. According to tradition, its most famous pupil was Judah P. Benjamin, a member of the Confederate Cabinet.

After the fire of 1838 destroyed Kahal Kadosh Beth Elohim synagogue on Hasell Street, the Hebrew Orphan Society offered its building while a new synagogue was built. Departing from traditional Jewish worship, the new synagogue featured an organ in the gallery. It was the birthplace of Reform Judaism in America. Both

Interior of Beth Elohim. Courtesy College of Charleston, Addlestone Library, Special Collections, Waddell Collection.

Jews and gentiles attended the sanctuary's dedication in 1841. They sang hymns composed by poet Penina Moïse and heard the Reverend Gustavus Poznanski say, "this synagogue is our temple, this city our Jerusalem, this happy land, our Palestine."

The Hebrew Orphan Society building was used as a hospital during the Civil War and fell on hard times afterwards. By 1931, the building was no longer used for the care of orphans and widows and was sold to attorney J.C. Long. Since then, 88 Broad Street has had office space for realtors and attorneys, residential space on its third floor, and a community gathering place in the basement bar known as the Rathskeller. When Long died in 1984, the property passed to his heirs, who sold it to Charleston County after Hurricane Hugo.

The Coming Street Cemetery

A pre-Revolutionary Jewish cemetery was located outside the city limits on present-day Coming Street. One of the oldest Jewish burial grounds in North America, it is the oldest and largest colonial Jewish cemetery in the South. Buried there are the remains of many notable Jews who lived in a community that became the largest, most cultured and wealthiest in North America.

There have been over 800 burials there, although many tombstones have been lost. The oldest identifiable grave is that of Moses D. Cohen, the first religious leader of Kahal Kadosh Beth Elohim. He died in 1762.

In 1903 Rabbi Barnett Elzas researched and published a record of stones dating from 1762 to 1903. The cemetery is listed on the National Register of Historic Places.

"View Along the East Battery", 1831, by Samuel Barnard. The painting shows the Holmes House (far left) which was demolished after the 1911 hurricane, and next to it the Edmondston-Alston House, before it was remodeled ca. 1838, and the Battery promenade on the right, before it was raised to its current height. Courtesy Yale University Art Gallery.

A New Era

**Century of Charleston's Greatest
Triumphs and Tragedies**

Pomp and Circumstance

In 1791 President George Washington made a goodwill tour of the South which included a visit to Charleston from May 2 to 9. His visit set the stage for celebrating the visits of President James Monroe and the Marquis de Lafayette who came to Charleston in the early years of the nation.

On his way to Charleston, Washington visited Eliza Lucas Pinckney and her daughter Harriott Pinckney Horry at Hampton plantation near the Santee River. The women had just completed the addition of the graceful Adamesque portico to the plantation house. When Washington was told that the live oak tree growing in front of the mansion would be cut down to clear the view, he asked that it be saved. It remains to this day and is known as the "Washington Oak."

Eliza's sons had served with Washington during the Revolution. His esteem was so great for the family that when Mrs. Pinckney died in Philadelphia two years after the Southern tour, Washington served as a pallbearer in her funeral.

Hampton on the Santee. Eliza Lucas Pinckney designed the portico, inspired by the portico of David Garrick's London home, Hampton on the Thames, designed by none other than Robert Adam. Courtesy Library of Congress.

President Washington next visited Snee Farm, the home of Charles Pinckney, then governor of South Carolina. According to popular tradition, the president and Pinckney dined beneath a majestic oak before Washington continued to Haddrell's Point where he and his entourage crossed the Cooper River to Charleston.

Triumphant Entry

Washington was rowed across the river on the Custom House barge, manned symbolically by thirteen elegantly-dressed sea captains of various ships in the harbor: twelve pulled the oars, and one acted as coxswain. At Prioleau's Wharf at the foot of Queen Street, he was greeted by Governor Pinckney, Lieutenant Governor Alexander Gillon, Intendant (Mayor) Arnoldus Vanderhorst, city councilmen, and the Society of the Cincinnati. Accompanied by an honor guard of German Fusiliers, members of the clergy, and other prominent citizens, the procession proceeded to the Exchange building, where Washington stood "bareheaded on the steps and received the cheers and homage of the public."

Charleston Entertains

President Washington was lodged in the home of Thomas Heyward Jr., one of South Carolina's signers of the Declaration of Independence. According to tradition, he rented the house because of concern that if he accepted the hospitality of any one family, others would be jealous. Moreover, in a city divided between Federalists and Democratic Republicans, his visit would not be seen as a political event.

Washington's daily schedules were full. He toured Fort Johnson and Fort Moultrie, site of the first Patriot victory in 1776, as well as the British and American siege lines north of the city. His entourage included his secretary, William Jackson, who had manned the lines and was captured when Charles Town surrendered in 1780.

The president was entertained every evening. On May 3, he dined at the Exchange and sat beneath a triumphal arch. Afterwards, sixteen toasts and speeches were accompanied by cannon salutes. After hosting an open house at the Heyward mansion, the next morning, Washington attended a reception given by the York Rite Masons before attending a "dancing Assembly" at the Exchange. On May 5, the Exchange was decorated for a concert given by the St. Cecelia Society, where Washington observed "at least 400 ladies — the number & appearances of which exceeded anything of the kind I had ever seen."

On Friday, May 6, the president attended a grand ball at Governor Pinckney's home. The following evening there was a dinner

George Washington, 1791, by John Trumbull. Courtesy City of Charleston, City Council Chambers.

at McCrady's Long Room sponsored by the Society of the Cincinnati. Washington worshiped at St. Philip's Church on Sunday morning and at St. Michael's that afternoon.

A favorite anecdote is that he could be seen exercising his horse as he galloped on Broad Street early in the morning. After winning the hearts of Charlestonians, Washington left for Savannah.

To commemorate Washington's visit, the city commissioned John Trumbull, considered the foremost portrait artist in the country, to paint a monumental portrait of the president. At that time, according to local lore, they didn't specify that they wanted the portrait of Washington in Charleston. What they received was a copy of Trumbull's portrait of General George Washington standing in front of his horse at the Battle of Trenton, a pivotal victory of the Revolutionary War.

Unhappy with the rendering, the city fathers refused to pay, forcing Trumbull to paint a second portrait. Several months later, he asked the city to send someone to approve his work before he finished the painting. The emissaries loved what they saw: Washington standing gallantly on the shore of what is now Mount Pleasant with the city skyline in the background. They paid the commission, but Trumbull told them that he couldn't send the painting to Charleston until he made a few finishing touches.

When the portrait arrived, they discovered that Trumbull had made some not-so-subtle changes. Washington looked the same, but the horse's stance now played a more dominating role. Its tail was raised in anticipation of what is colloquially called "the line of fire." The view of Charleston harbor was partially obscured by Washington and his horse, and a barge transporting the members of City Council was positioned between the horse's legs. In the foreground, strategically placed between the horse's back hooves, were two men on horseback, one of whom was Intendent Arnoldus Vanderhorst.

Charlestonians nicknamed the portrait "Trumbull's Revenge."

Washington Square

In 1881 City Hall Park was renamed Washington Square. In the park's center is a memorial to the Washington Light Infantry. Made of Carolina granite, it is a miniature version of the Washington Monument in the nation's capital. Unveiled in 1891, the memorial is inscribed with the names of important military battles. In 1999, a statue of George Washington was unveiled on the base where the Pitt statue had been located some years earlier.

President Monroe

President James Monroe came to Charleston during what was known as "the era of good feelings" and the city rolled out the red carpet once again.

James Monroe, 1819, by Samuel F. B. Morse. Courtesy City of Charleston, City Council Chambers.

Monroe arrived on April 26, 1819, and stayed a week. He was accompanied by his Secretary of War John C. Calhoun, and was received by Governor John Geddes, Intendant (mayor) Daniel Stevens, and the city wardens. The president stayed at St. Andrew's Hall on Broad Street and dined with Governor Geddes at his Broad Street home.

Monroe was entertained at City Hall on Broad Street, the South Carolina Society Hall on Meeting Street, and by the Society of the Cincinnati. There was a "splendid concert and ball" given by the St. Cecilia Society, and a display of fireworks from the Orphan House grounds. The President toured the harbor forts on the steamship *Charleston*, receiving salutes at Castle Pinckney, Fort Johnson and Fort Moultrie, and toured the city's land defenses. On Sunday, the President attended services at both St. Philip's and First (Scots) Presbyterian churches.

To commemorate Monroe's visit to Charleston, city officials engaged Samuel F. B. Morse, inventor of the telegraph and artist, to paint the president's portrait. It hangs at City Hall in the council chamber; a replica is in the Blue Room of the White House.

General Lafayette

When General Lafayette visited Charleston a second time in 1825, many of the festivities took place on Broad Street. The Marquis, at the age of nineteen, first arrived in 1777 to volunteer in the American Revolution. He visited with Major Benjamin Huger in South Carolina before proceeding to Philadelphia to join Washington and his army.

With the fiftieth anniversary of the nation approaching, President James Monroe invited Lafayette to tour the United States. He arrived in Charleston on Monday, March 14, 1825. He rode in a landau drawn by four grey horses, accompanied by officials in other carriages and an honor guard. Place of honor, nearest the general's carriage, went to the French Fusiliers wearing the National Guard of Paris uniform that Lafayette had worn in the 1790s.

At City Hall, Intendant Samuel Prioleau greeted Lafayette and showed him the Council Chamber. The procession then toured the city. As they passed the State House (Court House), a miniature of the frigate *Constitution* fired a salute. The tour ended at the St. Andrew's Society Hall on Broad Street, where Lafayette and companions were housed. Lafayette also received visitors at the hall, including the famous Baptist preacher, the Reverend Doctor Richard Furman, and the Right Reverend John England, the Catholic bishop of Charleston.

Lafayette by Ary Sheffer, 1824. Courtesy Library of Congress.

Lafayette attended two events at the Charleston Theatre on Broad Street. During a theatrical performance, a transparency of Lafayette painted by Rembrandt Peale was exhibited. On another evening there was a grand ball at the theater, which was lavishly decorated by M. Sera, who had decorated a theater in Bordeaux for a visit by Napoleon.

General Lafayette attended a dinner for 250 guests at City Hall. Mordecai Cohen, who lived at 119 Broad Street, loaned his gold dinner service. Other entertainments included a pyrotechnic display, with an image of Lafayette directing a battle. He attended a dinner given by the Society of the Cincinnati, whose president was an old friend, General Thomas Pinckney. In Charleston style, many toasts were drunk.

On March 17 Lafayette departed on the steamboat *Henry Schultz* amid gun salutes. The general's baggage contained a South Carolina map in a silver case, presented by Governor Richard Manning. The map case, by Charleston silversmith Louis Boudo, is in the Metropolitan Museum of Art.

Lafayette's Long Name

At birth, Lafayette was named Marie Joseph Paul Yves Roch Gilbert du Motier de La Fayette. He wrote in his autobiography, "It's not my fault. I was baptized like a Spaniard, with the name of every conceivable saint who might offer me more protection in battle."

First de jure Marine Corps Commandant

O nce located on the lot of 71 Broad Street was the elegant black cypress town house of Justice William Burrows, built in 1772-74. Behind the house were a two-storied kitchen, a brick carriage house and stable with slave quarters, and a large cistern.

William Burrows Mansion, 71 Broad Street. Courtesy The Charleston Museum.

Justice Burrows died in 1784. His son William Ward Burrows was then living in Philadelphia and sold the mansion to Postmaster Thomas Hall, who had fought at Fort Moultrie during the Revolution and was imprisoned in St. Augustine when the British occupied Charles Town.

When Hall died in 1815, Jehu Jones, "a free person of color" and slaveholder, purchased the property and converted it into the Jones Hotel. In 1809 he had operated in the Moultrie house, located to the west of the Burrows house. In 1816 he sold it to St. Michael's Church, which demolished the building to extend the east churchyard.

The Jones Hotel was noted for its elegance. Thomas Hamilton stayed there in 1832 and wrote, "Every Englishman who visits Charleston will, if he be wise, direct his baggage to Jones' hotel." Famous guests included artist Samuel F.B. Morse, architect William Jay and English actress Fanny Kemble.

After several changes in ownership, the house become a rental property. It was badly neglected, and by 1928 it was condemned. It was purchased by a buyer who planned to rebuild the mansion on the Ashley River. The building was dismantled, but the Great Depression intervened, and the architectural elements languished in storage for three decades. In 1959 they were purchased by Henry Francis du Pont, who installed them in the Charleston room at Winterthur Museum in Delaware.

Justice William Burrows

William Burrows emigrated from England in 1741 when he was about fouirteen years old. Nobody knows his origins. Within thirty years he had acquired more than 10,000 acres in Berkeley, Colleton, and Craven counties and enjoyed a country seat at Magnolia Umbra plantation on Charles Town Neck (now the site of Magnolia and St. Lawrence cemeteries).

As his holdings had increased so did his social position. He was admitted to the practice of law in 1748, became a justice of the peace for Berkeley County in 1756, and continued to advance to master in chancery (1761), assistant justice (1762), and justice (1764). He was president of the St. George's Society in 1771 and the steward (president) of the St. Andrew's Society. He was one of the founding members of the Charles Town Library Society in 1748 and a member of St. Philip's Church. When the parish split in 1751, Burrows purchased Pew 8 at St. Michael's and was elected to the vestry for three consecutive years.

The First Commandant

William Burrows' son, William Ward Burrows, is one of the Low-country's most distinguished natives. He was educated abroad and admitted to the Inner Temple at the Inns of Court, London, in 1772. He returned from England before the Revolution and served as an officer in the South Carolina Marines. He moved to Philadelphia and married after the war. When the U.S. Marine Corps was established in 1798, President John Adams appointed him commandant, with the rank of major.

William Ward Burrows, by John J. Capolino.
Courtesy U.S. Marine Corps Art Collection.

Burrows was the first de jure U.S. Marine leader to bear the title commandant. Capt. Samuel Nicholas, who was the commander of the Continental Marines during the American Revolution, is considered by the U.S. Marine Corps their first de facto commandant, although he did not bear that title.

Promoted to colonel, Burrows is credited with beginning many of the Corps' institutions, including the Marine Band, which was partially financed by levying contributions from his officers. In 1800 the capital moved to Washington, D.C. Burrows was a personal friend of Thomas Jefferson, and when he became president, the pair rode out on horseback looking for a suitable site to establish the Marine Corps barracks and commandant's quarters.

On New Year's Day 1801, Burrows marched his band to the White House and gave a concert for President Adams. Another concert was performed for President Jefferson's inauguration and another on the fourth of July that same year.

Colonel Burrows retired in 1804 due to failing health, and died in 1805. According to the March 28, 1805, *Charleston City Gazette* obituary, the commandant was the "most benevolent of men." Washington Irving described Burrows as "a gentleman of accomplished mind and polished manners." Burrows was buried in the Presbyterian Cemetery in Washington, D.C. When Arlington National Cemetery was established in 1892, he was reinterred there with full honors.

In World War II, the U.S. Navy converted a Grace Steamship Company vessel into the USS *William Ward Burrows*, named in honor of the first commandant. It was used as a troop transport and saw service in the south and west Pacific, 1940-1946.

The Assassination

One of Charles Town's most prominent physicians was Dr. David Ramsay. He was a founding member of the medical society of South Carolina, and became president in 1797. A paper presented to the Medical Society on the first day of 1800 made him the country's first important medical historian of the century.

Ramsay was born in April 1749 in Lancaster County, Pennsylvania. In spite of modest circumstances, his father had ambitions for his three sons, who were educated to enter the leading professions of the day. William, the eldest, was designated for the ministry and Nathaniel studied law. Brother-in-law of the celebrated artist Charles Wilson Peale, Nathaniel was also a Revolutionary War hero, a member of the Congress of the Confederation, and later served in the United States Congress.

David, the youngest, became a physician. He was precocious, could read the Bible at age six, and had mastered the classics before entering the College of New Jersey (Princeton) at sixteen. After graduation, Ramsay attended the Medical School of the College of Pennsylvania and graduated in 1773. In Philadelphia, Ramsay became acquainted with Dr. Benjamin Rush, a signer of the Declaration of Independence who was noted for his work as a physician and educator.

Armed with an impressive letter of introduction from Dr. Rush, Ramsey decided to move to South Carolina. He was described as handsome, muscular, and athletic with an eye somewhat damaged by smallpox. He was sociable, and it did not take him long to find a suitable wife. In 1775 he married Sabina Ellis, a young lady with a considerable fortune. But she died a year after their marriage.

As war loomed on the horizon, Ramsay became an ardent Patriot, serving in the South Carolina General Assembly from 1776 to 1781. He was an army surgeon at the siege of Savannah. After Charles Town fell to the British in 1780, he was seized from his home and thrown on a prison ship with other prominent civic leaders and exiled in St. Augustine, in British East Florida. Ramsay was exchanged after eleven months and continued to serve in the state legislature then meeting in Jacksonboro.

In 1783 he married Frances Witherspoon, daughter of John Witherspoon, a New Jersey signer of the Declaration of Independence and president of the College of New Jersey (now Princeton University). The newlyweds purchased 92 Broad Street, a house that Ramsay would occupy until his death. Frances Ramsay died shortly after giving birth to a son a year later.

The Patriot

Henry Laurens. Courtesy Library of Congress.

Ramsay served in the Congress of the Confederation, 1782-1786, and as president pro tempore in John Hancock's absence in 1785-86. He returned to Charleston to write a history of the Revolution. He sought out Henry Laurens, once president of the Continental Congress.

In 1787, Ramsay married Laurens' daughter Martha in a quiet ceremony at Mepkin plantation. This match enabled Ramsay to pursue historical works with vigor. Martha Laurens was related by marriage to Gov. Charles Pinckney; Ralph Izard; John Rutledge; Arthur Middleton, a South Carolina signer of the Declaration of Independence; Daniel Huger, a delegate to the Continental Congress and later U.S. congressman; and Lewis Morris, a New York signer of the Declaration of Independence.

Writing historical works consumed much of Ramsay's time. He published *History of the Revolution of South Carolina*, *History of the American Revolution*, *Life of Washington*, and a *History of South Carolina*. He is considered one of the first major historians of the American Revolution. He is noted for a 1787 tract outlining why South Carolinians should ratify the Constitution. Other works included *Memoirs of Martha Laurens Ramsay*.

Ramsay was elected to the South Carolina Senate and served as president in the 1790s. When he invested his wife's inheritance in the Santee Canal and other visionary enterprises, her fortune was lost. It was amazing that creditors permitted the family to remain in their home.

Shot on Broad Street

Ramsay was court-appointed to examine a tailor named William Linnen, who was known for serial litigation and nuisance lawsuits. After Linnen attempted to murder his attorney, Ramsay reported that the man was deranged and it would be dangerous to let him go at large.

When Linnen was released, he threatened Ramsay, who did not take it seriously. In the afternoon of May 6, 1815, Ramsay passed Linnen on Broad Street. Linnen removed a "horseman's pistol" he had concealed in a handkerchief and shot Ramsay twice in the back and once in the hip. The doctor was carried home, insisting that Linnen was insane and could not be held responsible for his act.

Ramsay died on May 8 and was buried in the Circular Congregational churchyard. He was survived by four daughters and four sons. There were eleven children, three of whom died young. His estate was valueless. The three unmarried daughters opened a school at 92 Broad Street, and the family managed as best they could.

92 Broad Street is believed to have been built about 1740 by Solomon Legare for his daughter Mary Legare Ellis. Courtesy Library of Congress.

The Phrenologist and the Skeptic

Clark Mills developed his art in his studio at 51 Broad Street before becoming one of America's most prominent sculptors. The self-taught Mills pioneered new techniques in bronze casting, built his own foundry, and succeeded in an area where he had no formal training. His meteoric rise to national prominence started on the streets of Charleston.

Clark Mills' studio at 51 Broad Street. Courtesy Library of Congress.

Mills was born in Onondaga County, New York in 1810. When his father died, young Mills was sent to live with his uncle. He ran away at the age of thirteen and wandered to cities as far-flung as Syracuse and New Orleans, working as a teamster, lumberjack, farmhand, carpenter, and millwright. After getting frostbite from cutting timber in a swamp, Mills moved to Charleston and vowed never to work again as a common laborer.

Charleston was noted for its wealth, sophistication, and patronage of the fine arts. Many prominent citizens had traveled abroad and wanted to replicate what they saw in their homes and churches. To take advantage of those desires, Mills trained first as a cabinet-maker and then as an ornamental plasterer.

The Phrenologist

Mills lived in relative obscurity until a chance encounter with a phrenologist changed the course of his life. Phrenology exerted an influence on American society in Victorian times, somewhat comparable to the influence of psychology in modern times. Roughly defined, phrenology is based on the belief that certain mental faculties and character traits are indicated by configurations of the skull.

Mills' remarkable story has been preserved because of an interview that was published over a century ago. As Mills told it, he was employed as a plasterer who supplemented his income with bear baiting. While walking to work one morning, Mills passed a phrenologist's shop. Outside was a sign that promised skeptics would not be charged for an examination of their heads. Intrigued, he decided to investigate.

After the examination, the phrenologist told Mills that he had the organ of sculpture in an eminent degree, and if he were to cultivate this rare and valuable talent, he would be a very distinguished artist. To which Mills replied, "I never had any confidence in your pretend science, but if I did, your account of my head would utterly destroy it. Sir, I am a house plasterer and know nothing about sculpture whatsoever."

But the phrenologist's words haunted him. Mills had never thought of trying sculpture and did not know how to begin. One day he saw an Italian carrying a plaster bust of Napoleon and asked him to show how it was molded. The Italian obliged, and Mills was hooked. First, he created a plaster likeness of his father-in-law. Everyone who saw it thought it was a wonder.

Mills kept on casting and soon opened a studio on Broad Street. The building had been designed as a double tenement, which had been occupied by Mrs. C.P. Huard and Erastus Bulkley. When Mrs. Huard moved out, Mills rented the vacant space. Mr. Bulkley next door was a marble agent who kept some of his supplies in the yard behind the house. With a ready supply of material nearby, in 1845, Mills made a marble bust of John C. Calhoun. The bust is now in Charleston's City Hall.

Equestrian statue of Andrew Jackson by Clark Mills, Lafayette Square, Washington, D.C., Courtesy Library of Congress.

By the time Mills had done a score of plaster busts, local patrons agreed to finance his studying in Rome. Coincidentally, in the late 1840s the nation's leaders were yearning for an American who could create a monumental equestrian statue for the capital city. Quite by chance, while visiting Washington, Mills met the Honorable Cave Johnson, postmaster general and chairman of the Jackson Memorial Committee. Johnson persuaded Mills to submit a design for the statue. The committee approved it, and the surprised Mills was off and running.

In 1849 Mills moved to Washington and set up a furnace and studio near Lafayette Square. After numerous failed attempts, the sixth recasting succeeded with Andrew Jackson mounted on a bronze horse rearing up on its hind legs. By loading the rump of the horse so that it outweighed the foreparts, Mills had created an engineering marvel that had confounded great artists and engineers before him.

The statue was dedicated on January 8, 1853, the thirty-eighth anniversary of the Battle of New Orleans. President Franklin Pierce, the entire cabinet, and 15,000 spectators listened to Stephen A. Douglas' dedicatory address and watched Mills unveil the fifteen-ton bronze on its granite pedestal.

Mills' foundry cast Thomas Crawford's Statue of Freedom for the Capitol dome. Mills continued to make history. On February 11, 1865, about two months before his death, Abraham Lincoln permitted Mills to make a life mask of his face. This was the second and last life mask made of Lincoln.

After the war, the prolific sculptor continued to work until his death in January 1883. In the 20th century, he was honored for his achievements when the U.S. Navy named the liberty ship (cargo) SS *Clark Mills* during World War II. In Charleston, his studio at 51 Broad Street was named a National Historic Landmark on October 15, 1966, and was listed on the National Register of Historic Places. A modest marker commemorates the honor.

Philip Reid

When Mills had moved to Washington, he brought with him an enslaved apprentice named Philip Reid. When President Lincoln signed an act abolishing involuntary servitude in the District of Columbia on April 16, 1862, district slave owners were allowed to petition for compensation. Mills petitioned for eleven slaves, including Philip Reid who was "aged 42 years, mulatto color, short in statue, in good health, not prepossessing in appearance but smart in mind, a good workman in a foundry." Mills asked $1,500 for Reid, but received $350.40.

Reid was a free man when he cast the Statue of Freedom and loaded the statue's five sections onto wagons that transported them from the foundry in Bladensburg, Maryland, to Washington. The statue was placed above the Capitol dome in 1863. In 1928, Reid was posthumously praised on the floor of the House of Representatives "for his faithful and intelligent services rendered in modeling and casting the Statue of Freedom."

Statue of Freedom. Courtesy
Library of Congress.

The Ground Mole Plot

The Bank of South Carolina was organized once the state recovered from the post-Revolutionary War depression. In 1796 bank officials purchased a lot at the northwest corner of Broad and Church streets, and construction began three years later. It was an imposing brick building with a raised brick basement. Set back from the intersection, the state bank was intended to dominate the business district where most buildings were narrow and sited flush with the sidewalk.

Bank of South Carolina, 50 Broad Street. Courtesy Library of Congress.

The T-shaped design featured an elegant pedimented façade with a slightly projecting center pavilion, keystone arches, and two niches on the Church Street side. The white marble belt course and marble window lintels further proclaimed the bank's status in the community.

In 1835 the Bank of South Carolina sold the building to the Charleston Library Society.

The Plot

Shortly after the Bank of South Carolina's completion, it attracted would-be robbers who made a daring attempt popularly known at the time as the Ground Mole Plot. The story broke January 10, 1803 in the first issue of *The Charleston Courier*, while slightly differing versions later appeared in *The Charleston News and Courier*, *The Times*, and the *City Gazette and Daily Advertiser*.

It seems that a horse dealer from Kentucky, a man named Withers (a.k.a. Weathers) brought his stock to Charleston to sell, but lost his profits gambling and carousing around town. Not wishing to go home penniless, he decided to recoup his losses by robbing the Bank of South Carolina.

Aided by two accomplices, Withers lifted the iron grating at the corner of Church and Queen Streets and entered the city storm drain. He made his way to a smaller drain in front of the bank from which he spent the next three months tunneling during the night. His only source of light was butter burning in a lamp. In time, he burrowed through the three-foot foundation and into the bank's interior.

All went well until the night watchman heard unusual noises at the corner. When a suspicious character was seen lurking around the bank late at night, the bank porter was notified. He searched the premises but found nothing. On October 7, 1802, around 11 p.m., a strange man was observed loitering near the bank. The police were contacted the following morning. Further investigation revealed a loose brick covered with fresh dirt. Beneath it was a package containing cheese and butter, a pickaxe, chisel, clothes, and a large hole with two legs moving in hasty retreat. Finding escape impossible, the "ground-mole" surrendered. His accomplices were arrested shortly thereafter. Because the plot had been foiled, charges were eventually dropped.

Interestingly, Withers' subterranean confinement later attracted the attention of the medical community who were amazed that he remained healthy for more than ninety days in the dank tunnel while unseasonable weather spread yellow fever and other ailments in the city. The story continues to be a Charleston tour guide staple.

The Charleston Library Society occuped the former bank building at 50 Broad Street until it moved to its new building at 164 King Street in 1914. The handsome Beaux Arts building was designed by Philadelphia architects McGoodwyn & Hawley. Robert Rodes McGoodwyn, partner in the firm, was married in 1910 to Kate Hampton Bryan of Charleston. Courtesy Charleston Library Society.

The Dueling Governor

John Geddes was a Democratic Republican (Jefferson's Party) who had a following among the city's merchants and mechanics. Perhaps this was because he was the son of Scots-Irish merchant Henry Geddes.

Born on Christmas Day in 1777, Geddes was twenty when he won office as a city warden. He climbed the political ladder quickly, being elected to the South Carolina House of Representatives in 1808. He was chosen speaker of the House for consecutive terms from 1810, until he was elected to the state Senate in 1816. He served as Charleston's intendant (mayor) 1817-1818 and was the first intendant to occupy the newly acquired City Hall building.

Elected governor of the state shortly before President Monroe made his Southern tour, Geddes was the official host, as his home at 62 Broad Street was the governor's mansion. (It is now known as the Confederate Home.)

According to tradition, Governor Geddes bore most of the expenses for the elaborate presidential entertainments. He was not reimbursed promptly, probably due to the financial panic that occurred later that year. After the governor's death in 1831, the General Assembly appropriated $3,000 to reimburse his heirs.

Geddes' Affaires d'Honneur

Shortly after he completed his term as governor, Geddes became involved in *affaires d'honneur* with the Simons brothers. Both duels are thought to have been caused by political differences. Geddes was a Democratic Republican, whereas Keating Lewis Simons (1788-1834) was a Federalist. In 1823 Keating Lewis Simons and the governor met on Sullivan's Island. Simons was wounded and limped the rest of his life. Geddes also fought Edward Simons (1778-1843). This time Geddes was shot in the knee while Edward Simons was unhurt.

That same year young Edward Peter Simons (1794-1823) was shot to death by Gilbert Chalmers Geddes, the governor's seventeen-year-old son. The younger Simons had studied law in the office of his cousin Keating Lewis Simons, who served in the state legislature and was a warden of the city.

Gilbert Geddes thought Edward Peter Simons had made remarks reflecting badly on his father and demanded a retraction. Simons protested that the father should demand satisfaction, not his son. Young Geddes posted notifications around town reflecting on young Simons' conduct, while Simons published his version of events in the *Charleston Mercury*.

The antagonists met at high noon at Fort Johnson. Each fired four times without wounding each other, but on the fifth round, Geddes was shot through both thighs and Simons was shot in the belly. Young Geddes recovered. Simons died the following day at the age of twenty-nine.

Governor Geddes died in 1828 and was buried at the First (Scots) Presbyterian Churchyard. He was fifty-one years old.

Truth is...

A persistent bit of local folklore is that Geddes needed to sell his properties on Broad Street because he was near bankruptcy after Monroe's visit. But actually, he was not in financial duress. In 1823 and 1824, Geddes went on a buying spree. Records indicate that he purchased several plantations from his mother-in-law's estate as well as several plantations from sheriff's sales.

Geddes sold his Broad Street properties in 1825. In addition to the Confederate Home property, Geddes sold two halves of the building next-door, now known as 56-58 Broad Street, both of which he acquired from his father-in-law, Gilbert Chalmers, in separate transactions dated 1798 and 1803.

Lynch Men and the Postmaster

Postmaster Alfred Huger was a respected member of Charleston's planter aristocracy who took his responsibilities seriously. His country seat was in St. Thomas' and St. Denis' Parish, now part of Berkeley County, at the plantation originally known as Pompion Hill. Huger purchased the property from Nathaniel Heyward in 1823 and changed the name to Longwood.

After graduating from Princeton, young Alfred Huger returned to Charleston and studied law. He served in the South Carolina Senate from 1818 to 1833. An opponent of nullification, he was appointed postmaster by Andrew Jackson in December 1834.

The Lynch Men

At the time Alfred Huger was appointed postmaster, slavery was a hot topic in Charleston. On July 29, 1835, the steamer *Columbia* arrived in Charleston bringing mail sacks full of abolitionist tracts addressed to city leaders. But Postmaster Huger set the abolitionist mail aside. That night a group called "Lynch Men" broke into the post office and stole the mail.

The Lynch Men raid the U.S. Post Office in Charleston, July 1835. A sign on the wall, "$20,000 Reward for Tappan," referred to a bounty on the head of Arthur Tappan, founder and president of the American Anti-Slavery Society, which was responsible for the mailing. Courtesy Library of Congress.

The next night, the group led a "celebration" with almost 2,000 cheering spectators and burned the purloined mail, along with effigies of Northern abolitionists, in front of the Old Citadel on Boundary (now Calhoun) Street.

According to popular tradition, when another group came for abolitionist mail, they were met by Postmaster Huger, who was armed with a shotgun and prepared to die before permitting another outrage. The mob dispersed.

Huger wrote Postmaster General Amos Kendall and New York Postmaster Samuel L. Gouverneur (the items had been mailed from New York City) that nothing could have stopped the offended citizens from seizing the abolitionist mail. The postmaster general's reply downplayed federal postal laws in favor of states' rights. Kendall noted that although Huger was a federally appointed postmaster, he owed a higher allegiance to his community, saying that "if the former be perverted to destroy the latter, it is patriotism to disregard them."

The American Antislavery Society's mail campaign was attacked by politicians across the South, as well as by sympathetic Northern leaders. In his message to Congress that year, President Andrew Jackson sought legislation to prohibit abolitionist groups from using the postal system to deliver their message south.

During Huger's time as postmaster, the greatest change in mail service occurred when letter carriers began delivering mail to Charleston residents. This service was provided by bonded contract carriers. For a fee of a penny per letter in addition to the regular charge, the "penny post" was born and greatly improved mail delivery. Another innovation that began in 1847 was the creation of the first United States postage stamps.

Confederacy Years

Unionist Alfred Huger did not resign when others quit their federal posts shortly after Lincoln was elected president.

South Carolina seceded from the Union December 20, 1860. With the termination of the federal post service, Huger remained as Charleston's Confederate postmaster. The bombardment of the city necessitated that the post office be moved, and by the end of the war Huger was operating from the Church of the Holy Communion parish house. Huger was so well respected at the end of the war that he was offered the job of federal postmaster. He declined because of his age.

Alfred Huger. Courtesy French Protestant (Huguenot) Church. Photograph by Richard P. Donohoe.

Watching His House Burn

During the Great Fire of 1861, legend has it that when Alfred Huger's Broad Street town house was burning, he pulled a chair into the street and stoically watched it go up in flames. He was one of the few property owners on Broad Street who was able to rebuild immediately after the war. His new house was a grand two-and-a-half-story mansion with a projecting bay window, an arched Italianate doorway, and piazzas facing Logan Street. Huger left the property to his son Dr. William Huger, and it was occupied by his widow after his death. In the 20th century, a family trust provided affordable rental rooms for young, single professional women. It has since returned to being a single-family residence.

The story of Huger watching his house burn has continued in Charleston folklore for generations. The late Margaret Simons Middleton, who lived only a few houses away, knew the tale and related it to her grandchildren. Her information is probably reliable. She was friends with contemporary historians and published four books about Charleston history. She was also named to the Roll of Honor by the National Society of Colonial Dames for her contributions to the community.

Postmaster Huger's home, 140 Broad Street, built after the Great Fire. Photograph by Richard P. Donohoe.

Calhoun's Catafalque

Former Vice President and Senator John C. Calhoun was one of the most powerful men in Washington at the time of his death. His rise to political power began in 1811 when he was elected to Congress and served until President Monroe made him secretary of war. He was vice president under John Quincy Adams and Andrew Jackson. He resigned as Jackson's vice president to take a U. S. Senate seat from South Carolina. President John Tyler named him secretary of state and he later returned to the U.S. Senate.

The car for a memorial funeral procession for John C. Calhoun (died 1850), and Henry Clay and Daniel Webster (both died 1852), held in New Orleans in 1852. Image from Historic New Orleans Collection.

On March 31, 1850, Calhoun died of tuberculosis in Washington, and because of the fear of contagion, his body was placed in an iron coffin. His colleagues held a funeral service in the Senate Chamber. Everyone who was anyone, from President Millard Fillmore to civilians, was in attendance. His coffin was placed on a bier in the central area around which gathered relatives and friends. His pallbearers included Henry Clay and Daniel Webster.

South Carolina Pays Homage to Its Favorite Son

News of Calhoun's death reached Charleston by telegraph, and as word spread, church bells tolled throughout the day. City Council unanimously passed a request that Charleston have the distinction of being Calhoun's final resting place, and the mayor contacted Calhoun's family. Once they agreed, preparations for the event started immediately.

In Washington, a committee of six senators was appointed to accompany Calhoun's body to Charleston, and they did so with all the pomp and circumstance they could muster. Calhoun's iron casket was moved by rail to Fredericksburg, Virginia, where it was received with honor. This was repeated in Richmond, and in Wilmington, North Carolina, where the casket was placed on the steamer *Nina*.

The black-draped steamer arrived in Charleston on April 25. Mayor T. Leger Hutchinson declared it a day of mourning and flags were flown at half-mast on public buildings and on the ships in the harbor. Residents respectfully shuttered their windows, and all business was suspended. Free passage on the railroads brought crowds from across the state to join in the mourning.

The *Nina* landed at the eastern end of Calhoun Street, and the heavy sarcophagus was lifted with great difficulty from the steamer's deck onto a large funeral car modeled from an engraving of one built for the Emperor Napoleon. The funeral car was drawn by six black horses, each attended by a groom. Moving to the beat of a muffled drum, the solemn procession marched through the somber city to Citadel Square where the remains were formally delivered to Gov. Whitemarsh Seabrook. A eulogy followed.

From there, a parade divided into ten components representing the state's most prestigious military, professional, scholastic, and social organizations, each accompanied by a marching band, made their way down Meeting Street to a black-draped City Hall. There the sarcophagus was carried up the steps and put on display in the Council Chamber. For the rest of the day, a steady stream of mourners passed the raised bier and threw flowers beneath the casket.

A state funeral followed. At 10 o'clock the following day, Calhoun's body was removed from the catafalque in City Hall and borne on a bier by honor guards to St. Philip's Church. The cortege proceeded up the central aisle to a stand covered with black velvet, upon which the bier was deposited. The Right Reverend Doctor Christopher Gadsden, bishop of the Diocese of South Carolina, who had been a classmate of Calhoun at Yale, read the holy rites. After the service, the body was borne by the honor guard to the church's western cemetery. The *Mercury* noted that the ceremonies absorbed the whole thought, soul, and presence of the city.

During the Civil War, it was feared that if the city fell, Calhoun's body would be desecrated. His tomb was secretly opened, and the coffin was removed to the Eastern Churchyard near the chapel. His remains were quietly restored to the original tomb after the war was over.

Truth is...

Some tour guides claim Calhoun was buried in the Western Churchyard of St. Philip's Church because he was a stranger to Charleston. The tale is based on an historical document stating that the Strangers Burial Ground was next to the Powder Magazine. But there were two powder magazines. The record actually referred to the Powder Magazine on Magazine Street, not the one on Cumberland Street.

Odyssey of the Hiram Powers Statue

S ome people confuse Clark Mills' Calhoun bust with a statue by
Hiram Powers done shortly after the artist arrived in Washington in 1836. As Senator John C. Calhoun was recognized as one
of the most important Southerners in Washington, Powers felt it
would enhance his career to do Calhoun's image. (Several marble
busts of Calhoun were made by Powers from a clay version for
which Calhoun actually sat. One is now in the Smithsonian and
another in the North Carolina Museum of Art in Raleigh.) Powers
moved to Florence, Italy, the year after he did the bust.

Hiram Powers' statue of Calhoun in City
Hall. Courtesy New York Public Library.

Powers was the protégé of the Preston family of Columbia.
John S. Preston was a wealthy planter, attorney, and state senator,
whose wife Caroline was a daughter of Wade Hampton III. Preston personally financed the first years of Powers' work in Florence.

During that period, Powers created busts of Preston family members and several other marble items that can be seen today in the Hampton-Preston Mansion in Columbia.

In 1844, the City of Charleston commissioned Powers to do a life-size marble statue of Calhoun. The senator helped in securing Powers' commission, writing that the sculptor's skill was "unsurpassed," and a plaster version was created later that year. The figure portrayed Calhoun wearing a Roman senator's toga. In an uplifted left hand was a scroll representing "Truth, Justice, and the Constitution;" the right hand was pointing toward the scroll. The cost was reported to be $10,000.

About the time Powers finished the Calhoun plaster rendering, he completed his famous work, The Greek Slave. The international fame of The Greek Slave proved to be a distraction and explains why there was a four-year delay completing the Calhoun statue, which was finished in Rome in 1849. Almost immediately, the Calhoun statue became an inspiration for the preservation of the institution of slavery, while The Greek Slave became a symbol of the abolitionists.

Powers did six identical versions of The Greek Slave, in order to send the statue on tour in the U.S. and England. Curiosity was increased by an air of scandal about it, a completely nude female figure at a time when women were covered from head to toe, and also a white woman with wrists chained together. Powers' third version of The Greek Slave, executed in 1846, was exhibited in Charleston as part of a tour of Southern cities. The Seravezza marble statue was exhibited in Hibernian Hall from December 29, 1851, to at least January 31, 1852. Art lovers could admire the statue from 9 a.m. to 9 p.m. at fifty cents per visit, or seventy-five cents for a season ticket. The third version is now in the National Gallery of Art in Washington, D.C.

On March 31, 1850, John C. Calhoun died at the age of 68. In May, Powers' marble masterpiece departed Italy on the bark *Elizabeth*. Also aboard the ship was Margaret Fuller from Cambridgeport, Massachusetts. She worked for Horace Greeley at the *New York Tribune* as its first full-time book critic and then as its first female editor. In 1846, Greeley sent Fuller to Europe as his first female foreign correspondent. She was a strong advocate of women's equality and became the first female journalist for the *New York Daily Tribune*. In 1848, she married revolutionary Roman nobleman Marchese Giovanni Angelo Ossoli, who in 1848-49, worked with Giuseppe Mazzini to establish a Roman republic as part of an effort to unify Italy. The revolution was short lived, however, as French troops, brought in by Pope Pius IX, quickly dispatched Mazzini and his cohorts, forcing them into exile.

Ossoli was left penniless and the couple decided to transit to America where Fuller intended to publish her history of the Italian Revolution. They booked passage on the *Elizabeth* and set sail for America. Interestingly, shortly before the departure, Fuller wrote: "I am absurdly fearful and various omens have combined to give me a dark feeling ... It seems to me that my future upon earth will soon close."

Soon after the *Elizabeth* left Italy, smallpox spread through the ship, killing the captain. On July 19, during a storm, the inexperienced new first mate thought he spotted the Cape May lighthouse off New Jersey. Sadly, it was the Fire Island, New York, lighthouse, causing the ship to hit an unexpected sandbar. On shore, the U.S. Life Saving Service arrived equipped with a lifeboat and a line-throwing mortar. They were unable to launch the lifeboat due to the heavy seas, and the gale winds, blowing shoreward, prevented all lines fired by their Lyle gun from reaching the ship's deck.

Later, a wave lifted the ship, smashing her in two. All the crew and passengers somehow managed to gather on the forecastle, the only part of the ship still above water. The ship was so close to shore that with a score or so of oar strokes, a lifeboat could have saved them all, but that lifeboat could not be launched. Captain Bangs ordered all hands to save themselves. Several of the crew jumped into the sea, leaving the rest to fend for themselves.

Giovanni Ossoli could not swim, so the three family members clung to each other, trapped. In an attempt to save the child, the ship's steward snatched the baby from Margaret's arms and leapt into the sea and drowned almost immediately. Another wave crashed onto the hull throwing those still onboard to their deaths, while those ashore watched helplessly. Margaret and her family were lost. Fuller's death on *Elizabeth* was widely publicized by her fellow authors and feminist contemporaries and inspired the epic poem "Aurora" by Elizabeth Barrett Browning.

Calhoun's massive statue sank to the bottom of the sea, but nobody knew exactly where. Charlestonians were determined to save their masterpiece, and the search for the statue became a regular item in newspapers across the country.

The New York Times and *The Charleston Courier* reported that the U.S. Revenue Cutter *Morris* located the shipwreck about six weeks after *Elizabeth* capsized. Attempts to raise it failed until James A. Whipple, a Boston engineer, was hired. Whipple had made improvements to submarine armor (diving suit). Inclement weather and the size and weight of the box caused it to remain on the ocean floor until October 31 when the sea finally settled. Whipple lowered five one-hundred-pound grappling hooks to the crate, but they were unable to grab it. As a last resort, the inventor donned the submarine armor, braved the sea and personally put the hooks in place. Amazingly, the statue was still in its crate, and, only the top portion of the scroll with the words "Truth and Justice" and the lower left arm had been broken off.

The monumental statue was repaired and displayed in Charleston's City Hall. It originally stood at the west end of the first-floor hall. After repairs were completed, it stood on a pedestal in the recess near the stairs, as depicted in the 1858 photograph.

On April 12, 1861, Southern troops opened fire on Fort Sumter, and in time the city was bombarded daily by Union warships. The statue remained in City Hall until city officials shipped it to Columbia for safekeeping. No one knows exactly where Powers' masterwork was stored. Some accounts say it was in the courthouse and others say the old State House. The statue was lost when Gen. William Tecumseh Sherman's soldiers burned Columbia in February 1865. Ironically, the statue might have survived had it remained in Charleston.

Burning of Columbia, *Harper's Weekly*, April 8, 1865. Courtesy Library of Congress.

An Oligarch Conspiracy

In October 1860 South Carolina's governor was Charleston-born William Henry Gist. He was a states' rights advocate and justifier of secession. Before the election he secretly wrote the governors of North Carolina, Georgia, Florida, Alabama, Mississippi, and Louisiana to inquire if those states would join South Carolina in leaving the Union if Lincoln were elected president. The governors of Mississippi and Florida replied that their states would follow South Carolina's lead. The others were noncommittal.

Robert Barnwell Rhett, publisher of *The Charleston Mercury*, with offices at 4 Broad Street, was a "Fire-eater" proponent of secession. Rhett also wrote secret inquiries to Jefferson Davis and other Cotton state leaders asking if they would secede. They were not encouraging.

About the same time, Speaker of the House Alfred Proctor Aldrich, a friend and protégé of United States Senator James Henry Hammond, requested his opinion about Separate State Secession. Hammond was a controversial politician who had served in the state house and had been governor of South Carolina.

An outspoken defender of slavery and states' rights, Hammond had been asked to fill John C. Calhoun's Senate seat. Although he popularized the phrase "Cotton is King" in an 1858 Senate speech, Hammond had become convinced that most Southerners had no desire to leave the Union as long as their rights were protected. Feeling that Southern obstinacy played into the hands of abolitionists, he gradually abandoned his secessionist views and urged Southerners to make concessions.

The 1860 Association

It was becoming increasingly obvious that the majority of Southern leaders preferred to wait and see what Lincoln would do before calling for disunion. Wanting to protect their privileged way of life, some Charleston elites decided to take matters into their own hands. Enter the 1860 Association. Even today, their revolutionary activities rarely appear in history books.

The 1860 Association's members were the very cream of society, welcomed in all the best drawing rooms. Its organizer was Robert Newman Gourdin, of Gourdin, Mathiesen and Company. With offices in Charleston and Savannah, his firm specialized in marketing Sea Island cotton, a uniquely silky fiber that produced fortunes by selling it to Belgian and French lace makers and English luxury fabric manufacturers.

Gourdin grew up at Buck Hall in St. John's Berkeley Parish. He was admitted to the bar in 1834 and was active in civic affairs. Gourdin and his bachelor brother Henry, the senior partner in the prosperous firm, resided in a handsome South Battery mansion that soon became the center of a massive propaganda campaign designed to push the moderate Southern majority into secession.

Starting in September 1860, every Thursday night more than a dozen conspirators met at the Gourdins, where they dined and strategized. Among the company were its president, William Dennison Porter, an attorney who served in both the South Carolina House of Representatives (1840-1848) and the South Carolina Senate (1848-1865); its secretary-treasurer Isaac William Hayne, then attorney general of South Carolina (1848-1868); and federal judge Andrew G. Magrath, who had acquired most of his legal training under Charleston's staunch Unionist judge James Louis Petigru.

The 1860 Association disseminated over 200,000 doomsday pamphlets written by Princeton graduate John Townsend. An aristocrat with all the right credentials, Townsend's country seat was Bleak Hall, the largest plantation on Edisto Island, with 3,779 acres. Under Townsend's meticulous care, the plantation was famous for its prize-winning Sea Island cotton. Townsend attempted to fan the flames of Southern paranoia by declaring that submission meant ruin and would only postpone the inevitable demise of the Southern way of life through the Republicans' use of patronage and federal jobs to dilute the South's stance on slavery.

The Gourdin brothers secretly corresponded with like-minded Southern leaders, hoping to get assurances that their states would follow if South Carolina dared secession alone.

And the would-be separate state secessionists had a good chance of prevailing. Because of its archaic form of government, South Carolina was the only state in the Union where legislators had the prerogative of meeting the day before a general election to select presidential electors. The legislature met on November 5 and unanimously chose Vice President John Breckenridge, candidate of the Southern Democratic Party. In case Lincoln won, Governor Gist asked the legislators to remain in session until the election results were published.

Although Lincoln received 39.8 percent of the popular vote on November 6, he received 180 electoral votes, more than enough to elect him president. With all the Southern states having voted against Lincoln, the stage was set for disaster.

Day After the Election

Once Lincoln's election was confirmed, a far-reaching drama played out in the U.S. District Court at 23 Chalmers Street where Robert Gourdin happened to be the foreman of a grand jury. When Judge Andrew Magrath (pronounced Ma-GRAW) asked Gourdin to deliver the grand jury's presentments, he replied that the federal grand jury could not proceed and declared that the "ballot-box of yesterday" ended federal jurisdiction in South Carolina.

Given the probable secession of the state, Magrath replied that he must obey its wishes, proclaiming: "That preparation is made by the resignation of the office I have held. For the last time I have, as a judge of the United States, administered the laws of the United States, within the limits of the State of South Carolina. While thus acting in obedience to a sense of duty, I cannot be indifferent to the emotions it must produce. That department of government which, I believe, has best maintained its integrity and preserved its purity, has been suspended. So far as I am concerned, the Temple of Justice, raised under the Constitution of the United States, is now closed." After more oratory, he removed his judicial robe and stepped down.

Shortly thereafter, William F. Colcock, U.S collector of the port of Charleston's custom duties; James Conner, U.S. district attorney; and Daniel Heyward Hamilton, U.S. marshal, resigned their federal posts. Only Unionist Alfred Huger remained postmaster amid the scorn of his peers.

HON. JUDGE MAGRATH, SECRETARY OF STATE OF SOUTH CAROLINA.

Honorable Judge Andrew Magrath. *Harpers Weekly,* January 19, 1861. Courtesy The Charleston Museum.

Disunion

The South Carolina General Assembly met in session on November 9 to discuss seceding from the union. Although the debate was intense, the Senate voted 44-1 to delay a secession convention until January 15. This was a momentary defeat for the separate state secessionists who feared that the momentum created by Lincoln's election would wane if South Carolina waited for other states to declare.

Caution about holding an immediate secession convention might have prevailed had fate not provided the radical conspirators a windfall. The completion of the Charleston and Savannah Railroad had occasioned a celebration in Savannah on November 3, 1860. With a branch office in Savannah, Charleston's shipping magnate Robert Gourdin was among the celebrants. The patrician plotters invited the Georgians to a banquet in Charleston on November 9 and arranged a princely welcome for Savannah's dignitaries.

After the Georgians arrived on the new railroad, City Council escorted them aboard the steamer *Carolina* for a luxury tour of the harbor. When they returned, the entourage was driven in the city's finest carriages to the Mills House for a posh 200-person banquet. It was so lavish that *The Charleston Mercury* claimed that it would have satisfied London's Lord Mayor himself. Mighty shouts filled the air as the crowd grew more boisterous after each speech and toast.

The main speaker was Georgia's prominent Unionist Francis Stebbins Bartow. Part of Savannah's oligarchy, Bartow was a polished orator. He had graduated with highest honors from the University of Georgia in 1835 and went on to study at Yale before returning home to read law with U.S. Senator John Berrien. He married Berrien's daughter and became a partner in one of Savannah's finest legal firms. Bartow served two terms in the Georgia House of Representatives and one term in the Georgia senate. He was a captain in Savannah's elite Oglethorpe Light Infantry.

Bartow urged South Carolina not to secede because it made no sense for two sovereign states with a long common border to be part of two different nations. He added that if South Carolina did secede without consulting her neighbor, she had the power of precipitating Georgia into any kind of revolution that she chose. The South Carolinians were charmed by his concession.

"The Charleston Convention—view of the South Carolina Institute building, in Meeting Street, Charleston, S.C., where the Democratic Convention will hold its meeting during the present month of April." *Frank Leslie's Illustrated*, April 14, 1860. The Ordinance of Secession was signed in the same building on December 20, 1860. Courtesy The Charleston Museum.

But ensuing events changed the course of history. By sheer coincidence, Robert Barnwell Rhett had scheduled a mammoth rally at the South Carolina Institute Hall that same evening, November 9. After dinner, Gourdin and fellow schemers escorted Francis Bartow and other handpicked Georgians across the street to speak to an assembly of over 1,000 men.

Well-feted and more expansive, Bartow spoke again, and his surprising oratory electrified the crowd. He opined that if his neighboring state seceded, South Carolina and Georgia must become one nation. His speech was followed by that of Henry Rootes Jackson, a prominent attorney and prosecutor in Savannah. Another reformed Unionist, Jackson pledged Georgia's support, declaring that they must act without delay. The crowd went wild and demanded an immediate secession convention.

The conspirators lost no time in telegraphing the state legislature that Georgia would support South Carolina, and hired a special train to transport a deputation to Columbia, including the federal officials who had recently resigned. Arriving in Columbia at 2 p.m. the following day, the delegation from Charleston whipped up support. By 6 p.m. that evening, both legislative branches had unanimously approved a secession convention date of December 17.

During the tumult, Alfred Aldrich received Senator Hammond's response to his request for an opinion on secession. It was a well-crafted, thirty-five-page anti-disunion epistle. Although the editor of *The Charleston Courier* requested that Aldrich publish the letter, he suppressed its release, fearing that Hammond's anti-secession letter might jeopardize the legislature's recent reversal. Hammond was contacted and, despite his disappointment over not having his masterwork published, he reluctantly resigned from the U.S. Senate.

On December 17, the Secession Convention convened in Columbia in the First Baptist Church. The 169 delegates were the state's power elite that included five former governors, forty former state senators, and 100 former state representatives. The delegates debated, voted, and eventually passed a unanimous resolution to secede from the Union. Due to a smallpox rumor (some suspect it was bogus), the following morning they decided to continue in Charleston and arranged for an eight-coach train. Arriving at 1 p.m. the next day, they were greeted by enthusiastic supporters and a fifteen-gun salute (one for each Southern state).

The convention assembled at 4 p.m. at the South Carolina Institute Hall amid a crowd of about 700 spectators. After parliamentary procedures, they adjourned and agreed to meet the following day to draft the ordinance.

"St. Andrew's Hall, Charleston, head-quarters of the Wood Delegation at Charleston," *Harper's Weekly*, May 5, 1860. Courtesy The Charleston Museum.

On December 19 at 1 p.m. the delegates reconvened at St. Andrew's Hall and voted behind closed doors to draft an ordinance for disunion. After the deed was done, someone leaned out the window and gave a sign to the mass of men crowded on Broad Street. When they heard the news, they gave a mighty shout that was said to have swelled until it reached the roar of a tempest, spreading from one end of the city to the other.

The delegates assembled on the following evening for a public ceremonial signing. A solemn procession of delegates from St. Andrew's Hall entered Institute Hall accompanied by 3,000 cheering onlookers. The Reverend Dr. John Bachman gave an invocation beseeching the favor of Almighty God for a blessing on the great act about to be consummated.

The first speaker was Judge Magrath. He was as dramatic at Institute Hall as he had been in his courtroom, pausing deliberately while his comments were punctuated by a shout that later became known as the "Rebel Yell." Men tossed their hats into the air and the ring of triumph sounded on every tongue. Cheers grew even louder when Magrath announced that Senator Hammond had resigned.

The animated spectators cheered as each delegate was called forth to solemnly affirm his vote on that fateful document. After the Great Seal of South Carolina was affixed, David F. Jamison of Barnwell District, president of the convention, proclaimed the State of South Carolina a separate, independent nation. The ceremony lasted two hours. A jubilant crowd greeted the announcement with enthusiasm "beyond the power of the pen to describe."

Former Senator Hammond was not present at that momentous meeting. He had resigned primarily for fear of appearing out of step with his colleagues, especially Senator James Chestnut who had resigned the previous day. As Hammond watched the frenzy in Charleston's streets, he commented that "the scenes of the French Revolution are being enacted already." In his private diary, Hammond confessed that if given a choice between saving the Union and saving slavery, he would choose the Union. He added that the South was wealthy and powerful enough to protect its interests without seceding.

Others shared Hammond's qualms, but with the popularity of the secessionist sentiment, almost none dared to speak openly. The exception was South Carolina's respected Unionist Judge James Louis Petigru.

The Destruction of St. Andrew's Society Hall

In 1826 Robert Mills, in his *Statistics of South Carolina*, commented: "St. Andrew's Hall presents a neat modern front, in good style. The interior is well arranged, with a large handsome room on the second story, much in use on public occasions." Completed in 1815, the hall was designed by Hugh Smith, merchant and "gentleman architect," who was a member of the society.

Saint Andrew's Hall served as a meeting place for the South Carolina Jockey Club, the St. Cecilia Society, and the Hebrew Benevolent Society. When they visited Charleston, both President James Monroe and the Marquis de Lafayette lodged there. Daniel Webster dined there in 1847 when he was a guest of the New England Society of Charleston.

St. Andrew's Hall after The Great Fire of 1861. Courtesy College of Charleston, Addlestone Library, Special Collections, Waddell Collection.

St. Andrew's Society Hall was destroyed in the Great Fire of 1861, but some of its valuable contents were salvaged. The table and chairs where the Ordinance of Secession was drafted are now on display at The Charleston Museum. Several portraits and articles of furniture, along with the 1814 cornerstone, are in the South Carolina Society Hall, and records dating back to 1729 are in the College of Charleston, Addlestone Library, Special Collections.

St. Andrew's Hall was never rebuilt.

The Democratic Convention of 1860

St. Andrew's Hall served as headquarters of the so-called Wood Delegation to the Democratic Party Convention of 1860. Fernando Wood, Democratic mayor of New York City, and his hand-picked delegates were supportive of Southern secession and defenders of slavery because Southern cotton was important to the New York economy. The Democratic Committee on Credentials rejected the Wood Delegation in favor of the "regular" delegation sent by the New York party's Tammany Hall faction, who supported Stephen A. Douglas and the Union.

The Wood Delegation to the Democratic Convention meeting in St. Andrew's Hall. *Harper's Weekly*, May 5, 1860. Courtesy The Charleston Museum.

The national Democratic Party, perhaps hoping to smooth over sectional differences among its members, chose Charleston for its 1860 Convention. The South Carolina Institute Hall, later the scene of the Secession Convention, was the meeting place from April 23 to May 3. But the varying factions also held meetings at various locations in the city.

The Great Fire of 1861

On December 11, 1861 on Broad Street, the evening air was warm and pleasant. Suddenly the watchman in St. Michael's steeple gave the alarm. A fire at Russell & Company's sash and blind factory at East Bay and Hasell streets had crossed the street to Cameron & Company's machine shops. A strong wind was blowing in a southwesterly direction, and flames soon crossed to Meeting

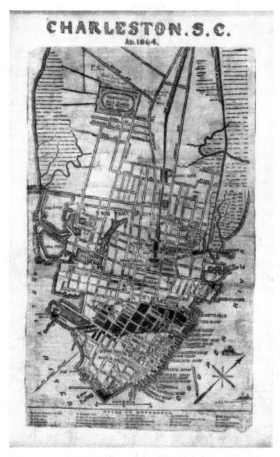

Map showing 1861 fire damage (darkened area), dated January, 1864, by Robert Knox Sneden. Courtesy Library of Congress.

Street. The Mills House was saved by staff who used wet blankets to smother sparks and embers blowing onto the roof and window ledges. The fire continued southwestward until it ran out of fuel near the Ashley River.

The next day dire tales circulated about the homeless and the loss of iconic buildings: the South Carolina Institute Hall and the Charleston Theatre on Meeting Street, St. John and St. Finbar's Cathedral, and St. Andrew's Hall on Broad. No lives were lost, but five churches and 600 houses were destroyed. The fire consumed 540 acres with estimated damages of $7 million, which was huge at that time. The overwhelming destruction forced insurance companies into bankruptcy, except the Elmore Insurance Company at 18 Broad Street.

Meeting Street looking north after the fire. Courtesy Library of Congress.

Many lost everything, leaving thousands of homeless people and others to roam the streets. The overtaxed military advised removal of homeless noncombatants from Charleston, although only a few left. Mayor Charles Macbeth asked those who had not lost property to donate food, clothing and shelter to those who were displaced. The response was heartening.

Northern papers were unsympathetic. *The New York Herald* commented that the fire must have been divine retribution and expressed the hope that it was an omen that foretold ruin of the rebellion. The December 28 *Harper's Weekly* opined: "Whatever the politicians and the papers may say, the Southern people from Norfolk to Galveston are sure to conclude that the negroes did the dread deed, and each man and woman is now quaking in terror lest his or her house should be the next to go."

Locals knew better. According to Lizzie Frost, "A good many persons think [the fire] was helped by the negroes and some think Yankee emissaries, but the fire took a very natural direction, following the course of the wind entirely — most of the negroes behaved admirably, our own servants and those of the neighborhood were untiring in their efforts to save everything, and to do all they could for us."

Broad Street looking west, showing ruins of 1861 fire (left) and bombardment damage to the John Rutledge House (center). Courtesy Library of Congress.

In the fire's aftermath, Fire Chief Moses H. Nathan established a fire-alarm telegraph system that helped firefighters locate fires more accurately. This eliminated the need for a watchman in St. Michael's steeple. It was the fifth fire-telegraph system in the nation.

Broad Street, looking east, after the Great Fire of 1861, showing ruins of residences and the Cathedral of St. John and St. Finbar. St. Michael's Church, seen in the distance, did not burn. Courtesy Library of Congress.

Phoenix Rising from the Ashes

The first Roman Catholic bishop in Charleston was John England, a charismatic and well-respected scholar who was consecrated in St. Finbar in Cork, Ireland. After his arrival in 1820, he purchased Charleston's favorite pleasure garden as the site for a Roman Catholic cathedral. Located on the northeast corner of Broad and Friend (now Legare) Streets, "New Vaux-hall Garden," developed by actor Alexandre Placide in the 1790s, had been a popular venue for entertainments and plays. Bishop England built a temporary chapel on the grounds and called it St. Finbar in honor of the patron saint of Cork.

Ruins of St. John's & St. Finbar's Cathedral, lithograph by A. Hoen & Co., Baltimore. Courtesy Library of Congress.

The bishop died eight years before the cathedral's cornerstone was laid in 1850. The handsome Ethical Gothic edifice was designed by Brooklyn architect Patrick Charles Keely, the leading architect of Catholic churches in America. Keely is said to have studied under Augustus Welby Northmore Pugin, the English Ethical Gothicist.

St. John and St. Finbar was the largest and most elaborate religious building in the city, boasting a nave fifty-four feet high, with side aisles twenty-five feet high and a tower crowned with a gold cross that stood 200 feet.

When the cathedral was destroyed in the Great Fire of 1861, *The Charleston Courier* wrote: "All of a sudden it was announced that beautiful architectural structure, St. John's and St. Finbar's Cathedral was in flames. The pride of that portion of our city was doomed to destruction, and its beautiful spire soon fell with a terrific crash, sounding high above the noise of the devouring flames."

Residents living near the cathedral had believed the brown-stone building was fireproof and moved their belongings inside. All was lost, for the cathedral's insurance policy had expired the week before the fire and, due to an oversight, had not been renewed. The fire also destroyed the rectory and 17,000 volumes in the seminary library. Only the gates and fence dating from the 1850s survived.

It took forty-five years to raise funds to replace the cathedral. The cornerstone was laid in January 1890, and the building was occupied in 1907. Keely was again selected as architect, assisted by Charleston architect Decimus C. Barbot.

The new Cathedral of St. John the Baptist, like its predecessor, was built of Connecticut brownstone. It is slightly larger than its predecessor and is noted for the hand-painted stained-glass windows made by Franz Meyer & Company of Munich. The rose window above the altar is copied from Leonardo DaVinci's Last Supper; the nave has fourteen windows representing the life of Christ.

Although the Gothic design called for a spire, the tower had structural problems that would not support a brownstone steeple. Not until a century later did technology allow the building to be completed in 2010. The base of the steeple is built of cast stone which weighs less than brownstone, and the spire is constructed of copper lattice, designed to be hurricane-proof. It is topped with a 16-foot by 9-foot Celtic cross. The steeple was designed by Glenn Keyes Architects of Charleston.

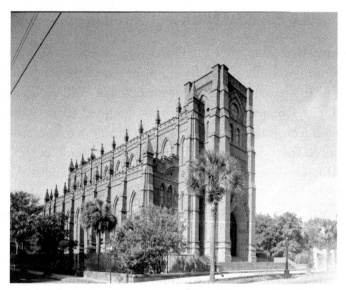

Cathedral of St. John the Baptist, 122 Broad Street, before the new steeple was added in 2010. Courtesy Library of Congress.

St. John's after the new steeple was added. Photograph by Richard P. Donohoe.

Stony Landing Block and "Stinking Stones"

Twenty-five years after the Great Fire of 1861, the Charles R. Valk House was built at 125 Broad Street, directly across from the cathedral. It was one of the first examples of Tudor Revival style in the United States. The house was designed to be earthquake proof, with iron rods running from the chimneys to the ground. Its buff-colored material is Stony Landing block, made at the plantation of the same name near Moncks Corner in the 1880s. An ingredient in the block was ground marl, so the block was a by-product of the phosphate industry in which Charles Valk was involved.

The phosphate industry began in 1867 and peaked in the 1880s with twenty phosphate mining companies in the area. Rivers belonged to the state, which collected royalties from the miners, but companies that mined land deposits made an untaxed profit. The industry revived family fortunes as members of the Charleston elite were presidents, officers, and superintendents of the companies. The industry also provided employment to freedmen and immigrants. The port thrived as Charleston was the world's main exporter of phosphate and its fertilizer. There was also a building boom in Charleston in the 1880s.

But a decline in the industry began in the 1890s because of competition from mines in Florida and elsewhere. It was compounded by policies of Gov. Benjamin R. Tillman. He believed the Charleston aristocrats were not sharing profits with other South Carolinians, although the riverine royalties paid almost the entire state budget. Tillman doubled the riverine royalty and placed bureaucratic restrictions on the industry, which was already in decline. By the early 20th century, most of the local phosphate companies were closed.

Broad Street POWs

Affter Morris Island, at the entrance to the harbor, fell to the Union Army in the summer of 1863, Charleston was bombarded continuously for 567 days, both by land and by sea until the Confederates evacuated the city in 1865. The O'Conner house, now 180 Broad Street, was located in an unprotected section of the city and played a key role in one of the more obscure and highly controversial acts of the war.

"Quarters of the Union officers exposed to the Federal fire in Charleston — sketched by one of the Officers," *Harper's Weekly*, August 27, 1864. Broad Street after the great fire of 1861, with the O'Connor house on the left. Courtesy The Charleston Museum.

With Charleston at a stalemate, Gen. Pierre G. T Beauregard was deployed north and Gen. Samuel Jones took command of the Confederate Department of South Carolina, Georgia, and Florida. By then Charleston had endured eight months of shelling and few buildings within range of Union guns had escaped damage. The following month, Union Gen. Quincy Gillmore was replaced by Maj. Gen. John Gray Foster.

Lacking the manpower to drive the Union forces away, Jones turned to drastic measures to stop the artillery shelling. On June 1 he requested that the Confederate government approve confining fifty prisoners of war in parts of the city that were still occupied by civilians but under enemy fire. Jones informed Foster of his actions and demanded that the bombardment stop.

Unfortunately, Jones' ploy backfired and set in motion events that would endanger helpless prisoners of war and outrage the highest officials in both governments. Soon, fifty prisoners arrived in Charleston, and five Yankee generals were locked in the O'Conner house on Broad Street. Outraged, Foster ordered that fifty Confederate prisoners be sent from Fort Delaware and placed them in front of the Union lines on Morris Island. The opposing generals sent angry letters back and forth, each accusing the other of wanton misconduct.

Charleston District Jail. Published by S.T. Souder, 263 King Street, Charleston, sometime after the 1886 Earthquake, which destroyed the tall octagonal tower. Courtesy Library of Congress

The situation was complicated by the fact that, since April 1863, the Federal government had refused to exchange prisoners to prevent Confederate soldiers from returning to fight. Ultimately, President Lincoln intervened and gave permission to make an exception to War Department policy. An agreement was reached, and the hundred Union and Confederate prisoners were exchanged in August 1864.

In early September, 1864, when the dispute seemed resolved, Gen. William T. Sherman's army captured Atlanta. When his troops neared the overcrowded Andersonville prison camp, the Confederate government transported hundreds of prisoners to Charleston over the strong objections of General Jones. Most were housed in A-frame tents crowded in a courtyard of the Charleston District Jail on Magazine Street, which was directly in the line of fire from the mortars across the harbor.

The Immortal 600

The Union general thought that the new prisoners had been sent to serve as human shields. In retaliation, he asked for 600 Confederate prisoners to be placed in an open stockade on Morris Island. They were transported from Fort Delaware and their captivity mirrored the living conditions of the Union prisoners. Prisoners were confined in an open pen for forty-five days, housed in A-frame tents. Their captors did not issue blankets, so the men were forced to sleep in the sand. The big guns would blast shells over their heads, and occasionally the rounds would prematurely burst, scattering the camp with fragments. The prisoners' meager rations often consisted of only two pieces of hardtack a day.

At one point, Foster had planned to exchange the 600, but Gen. Ulysses S. Grant forbade it. Only after Gen. William J. Hardee ordered the prisoners removed from Charleston to cities further inland were the Confederate prisoners transferred to Fort Pulaski at Savannah, where the captives' ordeal continued. They were crowded into the fort's damp casements and subsisted on a "retaliation ration" of ten ounces of moldy cornmeal and a half-pint of soured onion. The starving men were reduced to supplementing their rations with the occasional rat or stray cat.

The Confederate prisoners spent a miserable, cold winter there, thirteen of them dying of disease. In March the survivors were shipped back to Fort Delaware, where twenty-five more succumbed to illness. There they remained until the war ended. The harsh and unusual conditions of their imprisonment inspired one of the captives, John O. Murray, to record his experiences in *The Immortal Six-Hundred*. The name stuck. Sadly, using prisoners as human shields remains a dark chapter in America's history.

180 Broad Street fared better. The Greek Revival mansion had been built circa 1855 by George Washington Cooper and purchased in 1859 by Michael P. O'Connor, an attorney who opposed secession. During the Civil War, O'Connor was a lieutenant in the Lafayette Light Artillery and represented St. Philip's and St. Michael's parishes in the state House of Representatives. After Reconstruction, he was elected to the United States Congress. O'Connor's wooden house somehow survived both the Great Fire and the Union bombardment. After the war, the house was acquired by George Cunningham, Republican mayor of Charleston, then passed through hands several times before it was converted into condominiums.

O'Connor house, 180 Broad Street, where Union officers were confined under artillery fire. Courtesy Library of Congress.

Mayor Macbeth Saves the City

Charles Macbeth was elected mayor of Charleston in 1857 and served throughout the war. He discharged his duties with such discretion and good sense that he earned the reputation of being one of the most successful and upright of the city's leaders.

Macbeth was born and educated in Charleston. He was admitted to the bar in 1827 and practiced law with Richard Yeadon. Yeadon and Macbeth was as large and lucrative as any law firm in South Carolina, enabling each man to obtain great wealth, respect, and influence. When Yeadon retired, Macbeth formed a new partnership with Henry Buist. Macbeth was known for his integrity, conservatism, and loyalty to his clients' interests — traits that served him well in his role as mayor.

He married Henrietta Gourdin Ravenel in 1853. She was a great-granddaughter of the first Daniel Ravenel of Wantoot plantation in St. John's, Berkeley, Parish. He was elected to the state General Assembly twice and served as a member of the 1856 National Democratic Convention, which met in Cincinnati and nominated James Buchanan for president. He ran for mayor in 1857 and won after what was described as an "animated contest."

During Macbeth's tenure, the city witnessed the volatile Democratic Convention of 1860, secession from the Union, and the firing on Fort Sumter. These events were compounded by the Great Fire of 1861 that destroyed about one-fifth of the city.

The Fall of Charleston

In May 1861 the Union Navy began a blockade of the port. In July 1863 Union forces landed on Morris Island, and in August began the 567-day siege of Charleston, making it the most bombarded mainland city in the history of the United States.

During the siege, the notorious mounted Parrott gun, popularly known as the "Swamp Angel," fired thirty-six rounds of incendiary projectiles into the heart of the city before it blew up. As the Union troops under Gen. Quincy Adams Gillmore gradually took control of the barrier islands, those who could, left the city. The worst was yet to come. On February 17, 1865, Confederate troops began evacuating. It was a terrible time. Journalist Lee Cohen Harby wrote of the chaos:

"For days previous to February 18, stores were removed and ammunition sent away with each successive body of men who left the city. On the 16th, cotton was piled on the public square and burned, that it might not enrich the enemy. Tens of thousands of bushels of rice at Lucas' Mill on the Cooper River was set on fire. On the 17th, the Northeastern Depot, where large amounts of military stores had been collected and abandoned, was thronged with a motley crowd who took home provisions of every kind. As the day wore on, explosions were heard on every side."

Louis DeSaussure's residence, 1 East Battery, was damaged by flying parts of a blown-up cannon. Courtesy The Charleston Museum.

The Confederate gunboats *Charleston* and *Chicora* were blown up at their wharves. The "big gun" at the corner of South and East Battery was exploded, which blew out windows and doors and shattered the roof and piazzas of Louis DeSaussure's residence across the street. The following night no one slept; few even went to bed. Fires started everywhere, and black firemen put them out. They knew the end had come, that the white troops had gone or were going, and that the city was helpless and expecting its foe in the morning.

Not a case of outrage or violence occurred that night. Black firemen hauled the engines, put out the fires, and helped the whites. For whites, it was a terrible, heart-breaking, awful night. The men who were garrisoning Sumter had come over in their small boats, bringing their flags. In the early morning of the 18th, they were gathered in the city on the wharf, and there many of them wept aloud. Some prayed, others cursed; all said they would rather have died in the fort they had so long defended than have her ramparts desecrated by the Yankee army.

About 8 a.m., a terrible accident occurred through the carelessness of boys going back and forth from the Northeastern Depot carrying powder to throw on the burning cotton in the yard in hopes of extinguishing the blaze. The place was crowded with plunderers, people of all sorts and conditions, and as the powder trickled through the boys' fingers, they unconsciously laid a line from the burning mass to the depot, which eventually exploded. The depot was destroyed. Approximately 150 people were killed and another 200 were wounded.

The flames spread quickly and soon the fire was raging the length of Alexander Street, wiping out some of the best residences in Charleston. At 10 a.m. on Meeting Street the last group of armed Confederates to leave said their good-byes to weeping women who pressed around them. Yet many of the combatants were very brave and hopeful still. Few accepted the fact that the end of the war was near.

Ruins of the Northeastern Railroad Depot, accidently blown up during the Confederate evacuation. Courtesy Library of Congress.

In the midst of the chaos, some of the retreating soldiers animated by reckless patriotism planned to burn the city to the ground. So Mayor Macbeth sent Alderman George Walton Williams to the lower wharves to petition incoming Union officers for assistance. Col. A.G. Bennett of the 21st U.S. Colored Troops sent a note to Macbeth saying, "The troops under my command will render every possible assistance to your well-disposed citizens in extinguishing the fires now burning."

Union troops were greeted with great jubilation by the majority of the black population. Landing at the Cooper River wharves, the soldiers marched up Meeting Street and took possession of The Citadel and headed to the Confederate arsenal at Lynch (now Ashley Avenue) and Bee streets.

Residents of the neighborhood fled in terror to Christ Church Chapel on Rutledge Avenue after learning that a line of gunpowder was laid, a match applied, and a slow burn was headed toward

Hibernian Hall and other buildings retreating Rebels wanted to burn.
Courtesy Library of Congress.

the Arsenal magazine. But soldiers managed to extinguish the fuse. Other departing Confederate troops tried to burn Hibernian Hall and the Mills House by lighting a fire on Meeting Street near the State House (Court House) and City Hall. But thanks to Macbeth's intervention, guards were quickly dispatched to protect public buildings, warehouses, and mills.

"Marching on! — The 55th Massachusetts Colored Regiment sing-ing John Brown's March in the streets of Charleston." *Harper's Weekly*, February 21, 1865. After the city's surrender, Union troops were billeted in The Citadel. Courtesy The Charleston Museum.

Meanwhile, Union troops poured into defenseless St. John's, Berkeley, Parish. The Macbeths' Wantoot house was burned at the order of Gen. Edward E. Potter. However, Henrietta Macbeth had gathered valuable items she could not take with her and buried them. "Various methods were resorted to save jewelry & other valuables," she later wrote to a family member. "Among others, I took a silver cup, filled it with rings, watches etc., and buried it just below the middle of the bottom step as I sat there." Some of that silver is now on display at The Charleston Museum.

The Union occupiers allowed Mayor Macbeth to complete his term in office without interference. In 1881 the City Yearbook praised the mayor for not only protecting his fellow Charlestonians from the enemy but "even against themselves."

Charles Macbeth died in 1881 and is buried at First (Scots) Presbyterian Church. Wantoot passed through several owners before work began on the Santee Cooper Hydroelectric and Navigation Project in 1939, and the plantation was among those flooded to create Lake Moultrie and the dam at Pinopolis.

The Petigrus

When James Louis Petigru's story is told, the emphasis usually is on his opposition to secession, illustrated by his titillating quote, "South Carolina is too small for a republic and too large for an insane asylum." But the Petrigru story is more complex.

Though a Unionist, Petigru did not advocate the abolition of slavery by the Federal government. He was a Constitutional conservative, recognizing, as did Abraham Lincoln, that the institution of slavery was protected implicitly by provisions in the U.S. Constitution, such as the Fugitive Slave Clause. Petigru said that slaves should be freed by voluntary manumission, not by legislation.

James Louis Petigru, by Thomas Sully. Courtesy Gibbes Museum of Art/Carolina Art Association.

He was a slaveholder who lived in a commodious house at the southwest corner of Broad and Legare streets, on a large lot with extensive outbuildings, all destroyed in the 1861 fire.

Petrigru had a distinguished public career as judge, attorney general, and legislator. In the 1830s he opposed nullification and in the 1850s he was against secession, both on constitutional grounds. In 1860, he was distressed that his state became the first to secede. He did not live to see his slaves freed by ratification of the 13th Amendment.

James Louis Petigru Law Office, 8 St. Michael's Alley.
Courtesy Library of Congress.

Most of Petigru's contemporaries in South Carolina disagreed with his Unionism, but he continued to be respected and admired. After he died in 1863, his epitaph in St. Michael's churchyard was inscribed: "In the great Civil War he withstood his people for his country, but his people did homage to the man who held his conscience higher."

Susan Petigru King

Far more interesting than her distinguished jurist father was the winsome Susan Dupont Petigru. At the age of nineteen she reluctantly married Henry Campbell King, son of Judge Mitchell King, her father's law partner. It was an unhappy marriage, and when King was fatally wounded at the Battle of Secessionville in 1862, her cousin remarked that Susan had to "act considerably" in her mourning garb.

Susan considered the life of a Southern matron, where all but private thoughts were controlled by societal convention, stifling. She wrote about it in a series of successful novels. As it was "not done" for a Southern matron to author books and have independent ideas, Susan was considered "fast." But perhaps her most exciting adventure was outsmarting the Yankee soldiers who occupied Charleston after the war.

Yankee Extortionists

Judge Petigru had been a friend and attorney of George Alfred Trenholm, who was a partner with Theodore Wagner in John Fraser & Company, one of the leading blockade-running firms during the Civil War.

George Alfred Trenholm. Painting by John Stolle. Courtesy Ethel Nepveux.

Early in the occupation after the war, the Union provost marshal in Charleston threatened to charge Wagner with treason if he did not pay a $10,000 bribe. Not wanting to be executed as a traitor, Wagner paid. Sensing easy money, corrupt army officials decided that the head of the firm and a former member of Jefferson Davis' cabinet would pay far more. Trenholm was summoned from Columbia to answer charges of treason.

Trenholm and future son-in-law James M. Morgan brought a carry case full of $20 gold pieces. According to Morgan's book *Recollections of a Rebel Reefer*, the gold was checked at the station just before the men were met by Union soldiers. They were marched over to the Charleston Orphan House, which was being used as the provost jail, where they incarcerated Trenholm. When Morgan attempted to accompany Trenholm, he was struck in the stomach with a gun butt and left outside in the gutter.

The next day, Trenholm was taken in a handsome carriage to meet the military officials. When he refused to pay a bribe for his release, he was marched back to jail. Meanwhile, Morgan checked into a rooming house. The next day he obtained a permit to visit Trenholm. Morgan found him in a filthy cell. The only furnishing was straw strewn on the floor.

Trenholm quietly advised Morgan to take the gold to Petigru's daughter, Susan Petigru King. Petigru had died in 1863, and Trenholm had been supporting his family. Morgan went to the King residence, where he noticed that Union officers were in the parlor. Mrs. King received him and agreed to help.

Morgan returned to his room to get the money. As the streets were lawless at night, he was afraid to carry a portmanteau full of money and stuffed the coins into his clothes. Upon his return, Mrs. King excused herself from her guests and took Morgan upstairs to her bedroom. They pulled the coverings off her bed and Morgan unloaded the double-eagles from his pockets.

"While I was thus engaged, the beautiful lady standing on the opposite side of the bed was engaged in spreading them over the lower mattress. We then replaced the upper mattress, and I could not help but laugh when I realized the extraordinary situation in which I found myself, assisting a strange lady in the making-up of her bed!"

Mrs. King was laughing, too. She joked that the provost marshal, who had scared Mr. Wagner out of the $10,000, and the commanding general were downstairs.

Charleston Orphan House, 172 Calhoun Street. Thomas Bennett designed the building, ca. 1796, which was remodeled in the 1850s in the Italian Renaissance Revival style by architects Jones and Lee. The building was demolished in the 1950s, a great architectural loss to the city. Courtesy The Charleston Museum.

Mrs. King charmed the provost marshal and the commanding general into giving her a permit to visit Trenholm. While there, she could be seen sitting on the filthy straw weeping copiously while the courtly old gentleman tried to comfort her.

Author Margaret Mitchell, who knew the Trenholms, may have used Mrs. King's visits to Trenholm as inspiration for Scarlett O'Hara's call on the jailed Rhett Butler in her novel *Gone With the Wind*.

Mrs. Christopher Columbus Bowen

Mrs. King was often gossiped about. But her most scandalous action was marrying in 1870 the much younger Christopher Columbus Bowen, an unscrupulous Reconstruction politician. Bowen had a penchant for marrying older women, as was revealed in bigamy trials brought against him by two women in a New York court.

Christopher Columbus Bowen. Courtesy
Library of Congress.

Though Bowen was convicted of bigamy, Susan stood by him and used her friendship with the wife of Ulysses S. Grant to get a presidential pardon for him. Ironically, Bowen had been jailed in 1864-65, accused of plotting to kill his Confederate commanding officer, in the same cell in the Orphan House where a short time later Susan King had visited Trenholm.

Susan Petigru King Bowen died in 1875 and was buried in St. Michael's Churchyard. *Charleston News and Courier* editor Frank Dawson described Bowen as a "political agitator at once so bold, so unscrupulous, and so influential." He was Dawson's *bête noire*.

Bowen probably was the most corrupt politician ever to occupy the Sheriff's Office in the Court House on Broad Street. Indicted for murder and other crimes, he was never convicted, and kept his following among black and white Republicans. He was accused of paying voters, embezzlement of public funds, and other irregularities, but nothing stuck. As a U.S. Congressman, he allegedly sold an appointment to West Point. His true power base was the Sheriff's Office to which he was elected repeatedly. His political career ended with the rise of the Hampton movement.

Charleston's Constitutional Convention

The United States Congress on March 2, 1867, passed "An Act to Provide for the More Efficient Government of the Rebel States," also known as the Reconstruction Act. Congress declared that "no legal state government" existed in any of the Southern states (except Tennessee), and divided the South into five military districts, each to be administered by a U.S. military commander. (North and South Carolina together formed U.S. Military District No. 2.) The entire South (except Tennessee) was to live under martial law until all male citizens, regardless of race, color, or former condition (except certain ex-Confederate leaders), were permitted to elect delegates to participate in new state constitutional conventions. The constitutions were to provide universal male suffrage and had to be approved by the U.S. Congress. Each state had to ratify the 14th Amendment, extending civil rights to the formerly enslaved. Once these requirements were met, the president of the United States would consider readmitting the states to the Union.

The Reconstruction Act required a majority of registered voters to call for a convention. Large numbers of whites registered to vote but then boycotted the election, in a misguided effort to prevent the required majority. The tactic failed because it was the first election in South Carolina history in which black men were allowed to participate. Eighty-five per cent of black registered voters went to the polls and voted "For a Convention" and the required majority was achieved.

The Constitution of 1868 & South Carolina's Readmission to the Union

On January 14, 1868, the delegates convened in the former Charleston Club, on the west side of Meeting Street across from St. Michael's Church. The delegates were a mix of political newcomers and experienced veterans, with a Republican majority.

Seventy-six were black men, most of whom had been emancipated only a few years earlier; seventeen were black men from Northern states. There were forty-eight white delegates, fifteen of whom were non-natives. The twenty-three remaining white men included a handful of conservative Democrats, but most whites were Republicans, including Albert G. Mackey, a Charleston Unionist, who was elected president of the convention. Despite the black majority, white men were in control.

The Charleston Club House was across the street from St. Michael's Churchyard. It was designed in the Italian Renaissance Revival style by Charleston architects Barbot and Seyle in 1853, was set back 100 feet from Meeting Street, and reflected the wealth of the antebellum city. Formal landscaping included flower beds, meandering walks, and five elegant fountains supplied by reservoirs in the upper portion of the building. After the 1868 Constitutional Convention, the building was used as a federal courthouse until the U.S. Courthouse and Post Office on Broad Street was built. The classical masterpiece was shattered beyond repair during the 1886 Earthquake. The site is now a park adjacent the J. Waites Waring Judicial Center. Photo by George L. Cook, from *Souvenir of the Great Earthquake at Charleston, S. C. August 31st, 1886*, pamphlet, South Carolina Historical Society.

On March 17, 1868, the delegates adopted the Constitution of 1868 which was a remarkable departure from past legislation. It gave women the right to control their own property and to get divorced. It created a public school system that was open to all students, whatever their race. It shored up support of the university and mandated the creation of a normal school for educating teachers and an agricultural and mechanical college. It provided support for citizens who were blind, deaf, or mentally ill. No one could be imprisoned for debt, and men could vote and hold public office whether or not they owned property.

On May 22, 1868, the U.S. Congress ratified South Carolina's new constitution. In late June, the newly-elected General Assembly gathered in Columbia. Foremost among their duties, as specified by the Reconstruction Act, was to ratify the 14th Amendment; this was

THE LATE REV. B. F. RANDOLPH, OF SOUTH CAROLINA.—Assassinated Oct. 17, 1868.
[Photographed by K. A. Cooley.]

Benjamin Franklin Randolph, a delegate to the 1868 Constitutional Convention, was shot to death by three white men, in broad daylight. No one was ever brought to trial. Courtesy *South Carolina Encyclopedia*.

done. On July 18, 1868, President Andrew Johnson issued a proclamation acknowledging that South Carolina had fulfilled the requirements of the Reconstruction Act, and the state was re-admitted to the Union.

Tensions between Republicans and conservative Democrats erupted into violent conflicts. White resentment manifested in para-military rifle clubs and the Ku Klux Klan. In spite of occupation by Federal troops, in 1868 Republican legislators Solomon Dill, Benjamin Franklin Randolph, Lee Nance and James Martin were assassinated.

Gains Undone

The reforms of the 1868 Constitution were undone by the Tillmanite Constitution of 1894, which instituted a poll tax and literacy test to curtail the number of Black voters.

In a Louisiana case involving streetcar segregation in 1896, the U.S. Supreme Court ruled in *Plessy v. Ferguson* that racial segregation under the guise of "separate but equal" was legal. Jim Crow laws in the South would not begin to be changed until the 1960s. The 1895 Constitution remains in effect in South Carolina, although much amended.

The Hunkidories

The city Guard House stood at the southwest corner of Broad and Meeting streets where the U.S. Post Office and Court-house stands today. It was the city's center of law enforcement from 1769 until 1886.

The Guard House before the 1886 Earthquake. Courtesy College of Charleston, Addlestone Library, Special Collections, Waddell Collection.

The colonial Commons House of Assembly provided law enforcement for Charles Town with a paramilitary force called the Town Watch. The first Watch House was built by 1711 on the Half Moon Battery at the east end of Broad Street. In 1767, the Assembly appropriated funds to build the Exchange and Custom House, on the site of the old Watch House.

The same legislation provided for constructing a Guard House at the southwest corner of Broad and Meeting streets. Both the Exchange and the Guard House were handsome buildings designed in the prevailing Palladian Georgian style by architect William Rigby Naylor.

The design of the Guard House, which also contained the pro-vincial treasury, was depicted on a £20 note of South Carolina

The Guard House showing earthquake damage. Courtesy The Charleston Museum.

currency. Three thousand of the notes were issued in 1767 to pay for the construction projects. One of the rare surviving notes was sold at auction in 2005 for $3,737.50.

The Guard House, completed in 1769, was built by contractor James Brown, who was among the Sons of Liberty imprisoned at St. Augustine, along with other prominent Charles Town patriots, in 1780. Brown is also credited with building the first State House in Columbia — designed by James Hoban, architect of the White House in Washington D.C.

The City of Charleston was incorporated in 1783 and the City Guard, another paramilitary unit, was established. The Guard was reorganized as a uniformed paid police force in 1856.

When the colonial Guard House became inadequate to house Charleston's 160-man military guard, City Council in 1838 commissioned Charles F. Reichardt to design a replacement. It featured a six-column Greek Doric portico facing Broad Street and an eleven-column Greek Doric colonnade on Meeting Street opposite St. Michael's Church. The Meeting Street colonnade was removed in 1856 when it was considered an impediment to traffic.

There were large halls on both floors, a court room and detention area in the building, as well as quarters for the guardsmen.

The Guard House was destroyed in the Earthquake of 1886 and replaced by a new central police station on King Street between Marion Square and Hutson Streets. The U.S. Post Office and Courthouse was completed in 1897.

The only extant reminders of Reichardt's Guard House, other than photographs, are wrought-iron gates that feature swords in their design. Probably designed by Reichardt, the gates were crafted by ironworker Christopher Werner. They were never used in the Guard House, having been rejected as too expensive.

A pair of the surplus gates was acquired in 1849 by British Consul George A. Hopley, who installed them at his 32 Legare Street residence, which became known as the Sword Gate House. Another pair of the sword gates was acquired by the Military College of South Carolina and adorn the main entrance to The Citadel campus near Hampton Park.

"Dreadful Night" of Terror

The election year 1876 brought to the forefront racial tensions that had smoldered for a decade in South Carolina's Reconstruction politics. White Southern Democrats, with some black support, were determined to oust what was considered an extremely corrupt Radical Republican state government. White Democrats also detested the U.S. Army occupation, which included the garrison of troops at The Citadel on Calhoun Street for eleven years after the war's end. It was one of the most volatile elections in U. S. history.

Although some black voters were Democrats, the majority favored the Republican Party. White Republicans were mostly newcomers, known as "Carpetbaggers," along with some native South Carolinians, including Unionists known as "Scalawags."

Republicans supported the re-election of Gov. Daniel H. Chamberlain. The Democratic Party candidate was popular former Confederate Gen. Wade Hampton III. The political process was marred by violence as the candidates were backed by armed militia divided mostly along racial lines. There were riots and other acts of violence throughout the state, including Charleston.

The first incident in the city occurred on September 6, 1876. Radical Republican leaders were alarmed at the steady numbers of black voters enrolling in Democratic clubs. At a rally that night, a group of black Republican agitators called the Hunkidories and Live Oaks gathered their forces and mobbed the Colored Democratic Club on King Street. They were armed with pistols, clubs, and sling shots that hurled lead projectiles. White Democratic organizers in attendance were barely able to escort the club leaders to the protection of Union soldiers at Citadel Square. The white escorts then fled for safety as the mob grew larger and even more unruly.

In the pandemonium that followed, several policemen were seriously wounded and two newspaper reporters were severely beaten. Panic spread as whites feared that a race war had begun in earnest and blacks were in control. Twelve white men were injured, and another was mistakenly shot dead by a colleague. From that time until the election, the white militia known as the Charleston Light Dragoons patrolled the city every night to keep order.

After the Election

Throughout the fall, campaigning was intense, and there were abuses on both sides, including ballot stuffing and voter intimidation. In Laurens and Edgefield counties, more votes were counted than there were registered voters, with Hampton receiving the majority. Both sides claimed victory, with completely different vote counts, each giving their candidate a majority of more than fifty percent.

The day after the election, E.W.M. Mackey, a politically influential white Charleston Republican, gleefully read results from Republican newspapers to a group of black men assembled in front of a bulletin board at the corner of Broad and Meeting streets. Once finished, he proceeded to *The News and Courier*'s Broad Street office.

Mackey got into a heated discussion with a group of white men and an irritated drunk struck Mackey in the face with his hat. In the ensuing scuffle, a shot was accidentally fired. Blacks on the outskirts of the crowd thought that Mackey had been murdered, and in less than five minutes an angry mob surged down Broad Street. The men stormed the door of the Guard House, howling, "Give us guns!" But they were held at bay by Chief of Police Henry William Hendricks and a few of his men.

The mob, which included some black police officers, finally broke into the Guard House, snatched up Winchester rifles, and began shooting at every white man in sight. The first victim was Endicott Walker, a popular young businessman who was returning to work after dinner.

The riot was quelled when members of various rifle clubs, some of Hampton's Red Shirts, and federal troops joined ranks and took control. Two men were killed — one white and one black — and twenty-two others were injured — twelve white and ten black.

Rifle clubs functioned ostensibly as social entities during Reconstruction but their main purpose was to serve as quasi-military agencies of the Democratic Party. They proliferated when the Republican Party, along with black militias, were in power and federal troops occupied The Citadel until 1879. Ellison Adger Smyth and other Charleston veterans formed the Carolina Rifle Club in 1869. Hampton's Red Shirts were a more organized version of the rifle clubs, forming a brigade of about 15,000 men under central leadership.

During the contested gubernatorial election of 1876, President Ulysses S. Grant ordered the rifle clubs disbanded. So the clubs changed their names and posed as "baseball" clubs and even "sewing" clubs.

The Assassins

The riot was not the end of the Hunkidories. The state constitution required that, in a disputed election, the governor would be elected by the General Assembly. Since violence continued while the election results were being contested, President Grant granted Governor Chamberlain's request for control of Union troops in South Carolina. In the dark of night, two companies of infantry were posted inside the State House. The soldiers were told to refuse entry to Democratic legislators from Edgefield and Laurens counties, where balloting had been disputed.

By chance, a group of reporters discovered the troops' presence and quickly telegraphed the "scoop" to newspapers across the nation. Nothing like this had ever occurred before, and numerous newspaper editorials in other parts of the country expressed outrage that Federal soldiers were overseeing an election in the United States.

Hundreds of men had come to Columbia to witness the opening session of the legislature. When news that soldiers were occupying the State House and that certain Democrats were denied entry reached other communities, even more Hampton supporters hastened to the capital. By noon more than 5,000 armed and angry men converged on State House grounds, just waiting for the word to attack.

Governor Chamberlain and the Union soldiers were outnumbered and powerless to prevent bloodshed. Only the intervention of Wade Hampton saved the day; he stood before the angry crowd and advised them to disperse. Once order was restored, the

House Democrats convened at Carolina Hall and elected Gen. W.H. Wallace as their speaker. At the State House, E.W.M. Mackey was elected the Republican speaker of an assembly nicknamed the "Mackey House."

On Thanksgiving Day, Democratic legislators decided to take over the State House. Walking down several streets in twos and threes so as not to attract attention, they joined forces at the capitol and walked en masse through the doors without incident. General Wallace marched straight to the speaker's desk and took the chair. When Speaker Mackey heard the news, he rushed into the chamber and attempted to evict the Democrats.

Thus began one of the strangest episodes in South Carolina legislative history. On each side of the House chamber, two legislative bodies with two duly elected speakers simultaneously went through the motions of conducting business. Afraid of losing their advantage, both parties remained in the Assembly chamber day and night on Thursday, Friday, and Saturday. Pistols and rifles were smuggled in while armed soldiers were posted throughout the building.

Impatient for Hampton to be sworn in, his supporters gathered outside. Legislators representing both parties and reporters bedded down around 11 p.m. on Sunday night. Nobody knows for sure who warned Wade Hampton late Sunday afternoon of Speaker Mackey's plot to forcibly oust the Democrats from the House chamber with the aid of the unruly Hunkidories, who had been summoned from Charleston. Upon investigation, Hampton's men found a hundred or so armed Hunkidories, who had been sworn in as deputy sergeants-at-arms, hiding in committee rooms and awaiting orders. Democrats inside the House chamber were outnumbered almost three to one, and any confrontation would surely result in a bloodbath.

Governor Chamberlain did not order an attack, probably because he didn't want a shootout in the House on his conscience —

or in the national news. Years later, his authorized biography was silent on the subject.

Some citizens wanted to hold Chief of Police Hendricks accountable for the post-election riot at the Guard House, claiming he had protected the rampaging rioters. This did not sit well with some Charleston leaders, for Hendricks had been in Confederate service at Secessionville in 1862, Battery Wagner in 1863, and in Virginia in 1864.

By December 1877, roughly 200 men representing various professional, commercial, and industrial interests recommended in a printed pamphlet that Hendricks stay as police chief "for the good of the city." The pamphlet included endorsements from Confederate Generals Johnson Hagood and James Conner. General Conner had served from First Manassas to the end of the war and became attorney general of South Carolina after Reconstruction. Hendricks' commanding officer, former mayor and Confederate Col. Peter C. Gaillard, wrote a three-page letter on his behalf.

Hendricks was exonerated and went on to become the chief U.S. deputy marshal for South Carolina.

A Crusading Editor

Frank Dawson, an Englishman, was editor and publisher of *The News and Courier*, which was published at 19 Broad Street from 1873 to 1902. He was born Austin John Reeks in 1840 in London to an educated, upper-middle-class Catholic family. He took a European grand tour prior to his father declaring bankruptcy. An aunt offered to pay his university tuition, but she died shortly thereafter. So young Reeks took up playwriting and authored several comedies.

News and Courier building, 19 Broad Street. Courtesy College of Charleston, Addlestone Library, Special Collections, Waddell Collection.

He was a determined, romantic young man who became enamored with the Southern cause. He saw a parallel between "states' rights" and English efforts to establish the Magna Carta. He told his father he planned to join Confederate forces. His father declared that he would get himself hanged and disgrace the family name. So Austin John Reeks changed his name to Francis Warrington Dawson and volunteered for the Confederate Navy. But he became bored with sea duty, so he joined the Confederate cavalry and fought in eleven battles including Mechanicsville, Second Manassas, and Gettysburg. He was wounded three times and twice taken prisoner. He was promoted to captain in 1864.

A year later, when the war ended, Dawson said he owned a penknife and had only $5 to his name. He became a journalist at the *Richmond Examiner* before moving to Charleston in 1866. In 1868 Dawson and Bartholomew R. Riordan bought a major interest in *The Charleston News*, and in 1872 moved to 19 Broad Street. In 1873 they acquired *The Charleston Courier* and merged their papers into *The News and Courier*. Dawson was its editor-in-chief.

The News and Courier

During Reconstruction, *The News and Courier* became the most influential newspaper in South Carolina. Dawson opposed both Republican corruption and Democratic "Straight-Out" white supremacy. He promoted a "Fusion" ticket, of men he described as respectable black and white candidates to reclaim local rule. The effort was successful in 1871 with election of a popular local merchant of German descent, John Andreas Wagener, as mayor. In 1874 the Fusionists helped elect Republican Gov. David H. Chamberlain, who promised to reform state government.

Dawson wrote numerous editorials in opposition to political violence and lynching. He supported a state law passed in 1881 to outlaw dueling, and as editor, turned down hundreds of challenges. In return, Pope Leo XIII made him a Knight of the Order of St. Gregory the Great.

Crusading for the industrialization of his adopted homeland, Dawson advocated economic diversification, scientific farming, and other progressive practices. Pushing the slogan, "Bring the mills to the cotton," he did much to expand the textile business in South Carolina. He became a national political figure and was a delegate to the National Democratic Conventions of 1880, 1884, and 1888.

Dawson was a leader in restoring order after the 1886 Earthquake. Immediately after the first shock he left his home at 99 Bull Street and rushed to the newspaper office, which had been seriously damaged. Nonetheless, he and his staff managed to get a paper out the morning after the quake. Dawson also played a leading role in the relief effort.

In the late 1880s, Dawson initially backed the agrarian populist Benjamin R. ("Pitchfork Ben") Tillman. Soon, however, he joined the opposition against Tillman, whom he called a demagogue, racist, and opportunist.

On March 12, 1889, Dawson made national headlines when he was shot to death by his neighbor, Dr. Thomas B. McDow. Dawson had gone to McDow's office after learning that the physician, a married man, was pursuing the Dawsons' young Swiss governess. McDow claimed that Dawson had attacked him with a cane, so he shot Dawson in self-defense. McDow was acquitted of killing one of the South's most influential newspapermen.

A Woman Editorial Writer

Frank Dawson's wife, Sarah Fowler Morgan Dawson (1842-1909), was an editorial writer for *The News and Courier*. She used pseudonyms including "Mr. Fowler" so that her work would be taken more seriously in a paternalistic society. She is better known as the author of *A Confederate Girl's Diary*, first published in 1913.

The Freedman's Bank

The National Freedman's Savings Bank, established in 1865, was a visionary enterprise for the benefit of newly freed slaves. It failed in 1874 partly because of manipulations by Wall Street financiers. It was headquartered in Washington, D.C. and had thirty-seven branches, mostly in the South, with about $57 million in deposits. The Charleston branch was at 58 Broad Street.

The Freedman's Bank was at 58 Broad Street (left). 56 and 58 Broad were built by separate owners, and were united behind a common façade in the late nineteenth century. Photograph by Richard Donohoe.

Freedman's Bank records, now in the National Archives, include a great deal of information about depositors. Some were white, including Gilbert Pillsbury, a former Freedman's Bureau official from Massachusetts. He became mayor of Charleston in 1869, and that year applied for an account at the local branch. He served as mayor until 1871.

Most depositors were black. The average account held $60, drawing 5 to 6 percent interest, and were held by individuals, churches, and other organizations. King S. (Kinsale) Pringle was a typical depositor. He opened an account in 1870 at age forty. Pringle was born a slave at Drayton Hall on the Ashley River west of Charleston. He and his wife, Bella, also from Drayton Hall, were employed as farm workers by Edward and Arthur M. Manigault (grandsons of Charles Drayton) at White Oak plantation on the North Santee River in Georgetown County.

Edward Rutledge, who listed his address as 56 Smith Street, opened his account in 1872. He was a son of Edward and Rebecca Primus Rutledge. His mother, a nurse, also was a depositor.

William James Parker opened an account in 1870. Parker was a tinsmith with a shop at 12 Tradd Street, which he bought in 1873. Born in 1834, he had been the slave of Robert Forbes, a white tinsmith who had trained him in the valuable skill.

Charles Finley, unlike many depositors, could sign his name to his application in 1869. He was then fifty-five years old, had been born at Pocataligo, and now farmed on James Island. His son Neptune Finley, age twenty-five, a carpenter, opened an account in 1870 for his son John, then one and a half years old. Neptune had been born on James Island and now lived on Tradd Street.

The Freedman's Bank records at the National Archives are a viable source for tracing Black genealogy, as they often provide information not found in other records.

The Indomitable Matron

The Confederate Home opened in 1867 as the Home for Mothers, Widows, and Daughters of Confederate Soldiers. It was started by nine women and Huguenot minister the Reverend Charles Stuart Vedder. Available funds were one dollar given by a widow living in a charitable institution in Baltimore and money to pay one year's rent on the building. The rent was covered by Amarinthia Yates Snowden and her sister Isabella Yates Snowden after they mortgaged their family home at 15 Church Street.

Confederate Home and College, 60-64 Broad Street. Courtesy Library of Congress.

Initially, residents paid little or nothing, and by April 1868 the home cared for fifty girls. Within a few years, so many young ladies were involved that part of the home was converted into a private school and library. The curriculum included Latin, French, philosophy and elocution.

The Confederate Home purchased the property in 1874 and added a section with a cantilevered piazza. The board took over the former U.S. Court facilities in the rear of the building. The entire complex was badly damaged in the Earthquake of 1886. E.R. Rutledge, a New York architect, supervised remodeling in a Victorian version of the Second Empire style. According to *The News and Courier*, the slate mansard roof with dormers decorated with galvanized iron made the home one of the finest architectural attractions in the city. The renovations were financed with contributions from donors in the United States, England, and Scotland. A plaque commemorating their generosity is on the building's façade.

Many instructors taught for free, and the school prospered. In 1900, it was chartered by the state and a grant was given with the stipulation that the name be changed to the Confederate Home and College. When the school closed in 1923, it had educated more than 2,000 girls.

Amarinthia Yates Snowden

The driving force behind the Confederate Home was Amarinthia Yates Snowden. After her father died, her mother moved her family to Philadelphia so that her older children could be educated in prestigious schools.

After the family returned, Amarinthia attended Madame Talvande's finishing school and completed her formal education at Dr. Elias Marks' Academy in Barhamville, near Columbia. One of her classmates was Ann Pamela Cunningham, who organized the Mount Vernon Ladies Association and worked to have President George Washington's home preserved.

MRS. AMARINTHA SNOWDEN,
CHARLESTON.

Amarinthia Yates Snowden. Courtesy
Confederate Home.

Miss Yates had known Senator John C. Calhoun personally, and in 1854, she organized the Ladies Calhoun Memorial Association (LCMA) to erect a monument honoring him. They raised $40,000, and the monument's cornerstone was laid at Citadel Square in 1858. Before the monument's completion, however, war broke out.

Amarinthia married Dr. William Snowden in 1857. When war started, she was one of the founding officers of the Soldiers' Relief Association of Charleston, which raised money, clothing, and food for the Confederate Army. Her Church Street home became a hospital for wounded soldiers. After the second Battle of Manassas in August 1862, she and her husband traveled to Virginia to nurse 180 South Carolinians.

January 1865 found a widowed Mrs. Snowden in Columbia where she commandeered the South Carolina State House for a last-ditch effort to raise money for the Confederacy. The Great Bazaar raised $350,000, but it was too late. Sherman's army was approaching. Mrs. Snowden had met Sherman in 1850 when he escorted her to wedding festivities in Charleston. She asked for his protection, and he extended every courtesy to her and her charges. Meanwhile, Columbia was sacked.

Unknown to Sherman, Mrs. Snowden carried a considerable fortune on her person – the funds for the Calhoun monument. She had quilted U.S. bonds worth about $39,000 into her petticoat.

Back in Charleston in 1866, Mrs. Snowden organized the Ladies' Memorial Association, which held the first Confederate Memorial Day just after the war ended. As Confederate dead had been buried in Magnolia Cemetery since the Battle of Secessionville, the association made plans to get headstones for the fallen soldiers. The state General Assembly contributed $1,000 and agreed to donate granite and marble left over from construction of the State House. However, before the stone could be transported, control of the state government had shifted to Reconstruction Republicans. Undaunted, Mrs. Snowden went to Columbia and through her efforts, returned with material for more than 800 headstones.

In 1871, through the generosity of Moses Cohen Mordecai, Mrs. Snowden traveled to Gettysburg and arranged for the exhumation of eighty-four South Carolinians who had died there. Their remains were re-buried at Magnolia Cemetery. Mordecai was a blockade runner who lost his first fortune during the war. Afterwards, he moved to Baltimore and made his second one.

In April 1887, the LCMA celebrated the erection of a Calhoun monument by sculptor Albert E. Harnisch of Philadelphia, in Marion Square, as Citadel Square had been renamed in 1882. But the statue did not remain for long. The ladies didn't like it. Instead of four women symbolizing History, Justice, the Constitution, and Truth, only one disheveled woman was depicted in a subservient position, and even worse, the statue barely resembled Calhoun. Also, the statue, raised on a low pediment, was being vandalized because many blacks saw it as a monument to slavery and repression.

The LCMA engaged J. Massey Rhind of New York, one of America's most prominent sculptors. The replacement statue, raised on a high column, was dedicated on June 27, 1896. But Calhoun's strong support for the institution of slavery made his monument a target in 2020. City Council voted unanimously to remove it. It came down in August, 2020.

Mrs. Snowden died in 1898 and was buried with honors at Magnolia Cemetery. In 1917 the General Assembly and the United Daughters of the Confederacy erected a marble memorial tablet in her honor in the State House rotunda. Her memory was honored with plaques at the Confederate Home, on the Calhoun monument (since demolished), and on the Confederate monument at Magnolia Cemetery.

6678. Drill of the Charleston Cadets, Charleston, S. C. U. S. A.

The first Calhoun statue on Marion Square. Photograph by B.W. Kilburn, 1891. Courtesy Library of Congress.

Calhoun statue at Marion Square. *Sic transit gloria mundi.* Courtesy Library of Congress.

Isabella's Earthquake Diary

Shortly before the Civil War, Klinck & Wickenberg, a successful wholesale grocery and liquor business, opened on the northeast corner of Broad and Church streets. The founders were John Klinck, a native of Schleswig-Holstein in Germany, and Fabian Reinhold Wickenberg, a Swede.

The Klinck House, 134 Broad Street. Photograph by Richard P. Donohoe.

In 1871 Klinck's son, Gustavus, married Isabella Helena Strybing of Brooklyn, New York. When the business expanded in 1872, John Klinck built the newlyweds a lovely home on a large Broad Street lot. The previous residence had been destroyed by the Great Fire of 1861.

Built in the Italian Villa style but with Gothic clustered columns in the piazzas, the 4,500-square-foot home was designed to impress. It cost nearly $7,000, a large sum for that time. The architect was John Henry Devereux, the most prestigious architect of the post-war period. Among his many landmarks are Emanuel AME Church on Calhoun Street, St. Matthew's German Evangelical Church on King Street, and Stella Maris Church on Sullivan's Island.

Gustavus, Isabella, and their five children were living at 134 Broad Street when Charleston was wracked by the 1886 Earthquake. In 2003 Steven Holmes Semken, grandson of Edith Klinck Semken, Isabella's granddaughter, published Isabella's diary. In it, Isabella described their ordeal in vivid terms.

Isabella noted a strange atmospheric stillness before the upheaval. Sea birds, driven by a sense of impending danger, flew to and fro, while land birds started an unaccustomed chatter in the still of the hot summer night. Outside, domestic animals huddled together, while house pets sought comfortable assurance from their masters.

Suddenly, a strange noise resembling distant rolling thunder startled Isabella into a breathless terror. As the sound increased, she described how "the bed shakes; the thunder roars louder as the noise in the house increases and seems to totter on its foundations and rocks and sways like a storm-beaten vessel at sea accompanied by sounds of a ship's heavy timbers. The rocking of the building causes a nauseating sensation with a smell of sulphur and brimstone in the air." The children woke up, and the family hastily dressed and rushed into the street fearing they would be crushed by collapsing walls.

The sense of impending doom was overpowering. "No shipwreck, no fire at sea, no calamity on earth or water can be as fearful as an earthquake, when it is so violent that your house, your castle, your stronghold to which you fly for refuge and shelter from all the threatening damages suddenly becomes transformed into a dangerous powder mine that at any moment may spring beneath your feet and bury you beneath its ruins." Frightened neighbors had similar stories.

The next morning the Klincks saw that a chimney had fallen and crushed the roof above the sleeping boys. Plaster shards had fallen all around the room, but nothing hit the children. The clock, which had been thrown from the shelf and lay on its face in the hall, marked the hour when it stopped running: 10:55 p.m. on August 31, 1886. A neighbor's chimney had fallen into the yard where the children often played. Although their house was badly damaged from garret to cellar, the Klincks fared better than some, for they still had a roof over their heads and means to provide food for the family and other survivors.

Isabella concluded her narrative: "As I look back upon the terrible events of that awful night, I cannot refrain from tuning my heart-strings to a song of silent thanksgiving and exulting praise, and feel that the Great Earthquake was not a manifestation of God's wrath and vengeance but simply a grand and magnificent proof of His saving Power and Mercy."

The house remained in the Klinck family until Howard Holmes, president and treasurer of Tiedeman Company Whole-sale Grocers, purchased it in 1932. Later in the 1930s, Fred S. Poulnot, a pharmacist whose shop was inside the Lining House, lived there. The residence has changed hands multiple times since then.

Gustavus Klinck and Isabella Strybing Klinck. Courtesy Holmes Semken.

Broad Street Lawyers

The east end of Broad Street, between East Bay and King streets, was in the care of St. Ivo of Kermartin, patron of lawyers. In 1890, those few blocks of Broad Street sheltered ninety-five percent of Charleston's attorneys.

John Pendleton Kennedy Bryan. Courtesy National Archives.

Brothers Kennedy Bryan and George Dwight Bryan had offices at 11 Broad Street. They were sons of U.S. District Judge George Seabrook Bryan. The two brothers married daughters of Judge Mitchell King. George D. Bryan, who was mayor of Charleston, also lived on Broad Street in the historic William Harvey House at 110 Broad.

Julian Mitchell, Sr. was a law partner with Henry Augustus Middleton Smith, notable Charleston historian. Mitchell & Smith had offices at 31 Broad Street. Mitchell had resigned from his post as secretary of the U.S. legation to Russia when South Carolina seceded. A Confederate major, he was captured during the Gettysburg campaign in 1863 and was a prisoner of war for more than a year.

William St. Julien Jervey was solicitor for the First Judicial Circuit Court. His law office was at 14 Broad Street. In 1905, he won election as solicitor of the Ninth Circuit, defeating W. Turner Logan, the law partner of future mayor John P. Grace.

J. N. Nathans. The numbered photo was his season ticket to the South Carolina Inter-State and West Indian Exposition. Courtesy Charleston County Public Library.

Jacob Nathaniel Nathans, Sr., was admitted to the Charleston Bar in 1858. During the Civil War, Nathans served in the 27th South Carolina Infantry. His wife Alice Gertrude Cohen was a member of an old Charleston Jewish family.

Nathans and son Jacob Jr. practiced law at 15 Broad Street. Later, Nathans partnered with Huger Sinkler, in the firm Nathans & Sinkler. Sinkler had read law in the office of Mitchell & Smith, and later served in both houses of the General Assembly.

Blind Tigers

C harleston has long been identified with the copious consump-
tion of alcoholic beverages. Taverns were a mainstay from
the city's earliest days. Important events, such as the laying of the
cornerstone of the State House in 1753, were followed by a procession to a tavern, where appropriate toasts were drunk.

"Mr. Peter Manigault and his Friends," drawing by George Roupell, ca.
1760. The table is laden with bottles and decanters, some of which un-
doubtedly contained Madeira wine. Courtesy Gibbes Museum of Art/
Carolina Art Association.

During the Colonial period, Charles Town was the foremost import
and export port in British America for Madeira. In 1731 Carolina gold
rice was given an exemption from the Navigation Acts, allowing it to be
shipped directly to ports below Cape Finisterre, in Portugal and Spain,
two prime markets. The ships brought back Iberian wines — Sherry,

Canary, Port and especially Madeira. Much of it was re-exported, but locally Madeira became the favored drink of the elite. Madeira is the only wine that improves with heat, so prosperous Charlestonians built Madeira closets in their attics.

Two men standing outdoors with small still, one of them holding up bottle of liquor. Courtesy Library of Congress.

Things changed radically when governor Benjamin R. (Pitchfork Ben) Tillman had the legislature create The Dispensary Act. Thereafter, one could legally buy liquor by the bottle only from a government-appointed dispenser, of which there were only ten in Charleston County. The law took effect on July 1, 1893. The day before, *The News and Courier* reported:

"From early in the day until after midnight such another buying and selling of liquor as took place from one end of the city to the other was never before seen… Every man that had a spare dollar invested it in private stock, and why the whole town was not drunk for the next day or two no one has ever known."

Thereafter, Charlestonians resorted to "blind tiger," bars where liquor flowed freely. The ruse was that you paid to see a "blind tiger" (which didn't exist) and got a "free" drink. Charleston's "blind tigers" were listed in city directories as groceries, restaurants, drug stores, soft drink sellers, and even ice cream parlors. But they operated openly as saloons. Local law enforcement colluded with the illegal bars. Tillman and subsequent governors sent state constables to raid Charleston, after which the status quo quickly was restored.

Because the system became corrupt, the Dispensary Act was repealed in 1907, and replaced in 1916 by a "bone dry" prohibition act, three years before national prohibition became law. National prohibition ended in 1933, but South Carolina continued to enact restrictive laws. Only in recent decades has selling alcohol by the drink been legal.

The Blind Tiger Pub at 36-38 Broad Street is a reminder of Charleston's colorful history.

36 Broad Street. Courtesy Library of Congress.

"Bird's Eye View of the City of Charleston, 1872," by C.N. Drie. Courtesy Library of Congress.

Modern Charleston

Twentieth and Twenty-first Centuries

Captain Frederick C. Wagener

The Lowcountry desperately needed something to jump start the sluggish economy after the phosphate industry declined in the 1890s. Exports were reduced and trade with Latin America and the Caribbean was down. With the rest of the country, Charleston was affected by the economic depression following the Panic of 1893, which lasted until 1897. Hurricanes slammed the area in 1885 and 1893, and railroad shipping rates favored northern ports.

In 1899 railroad executive J.H. Averill suggested that Charleston could improve business by showcasing the area with an international exposition similar to those held in New Orleans (1884-1886), Atlanta (1895), and Nashville (1897). The idea caught on. Two early advocates were J.C. Hemphill, editor of *The News and Courier*, and Capt. Frederick C. Wagener.

The Wagener residence. In 1885, Captain Wagener purchased the ca. 1760 Edward Rutledge House at 117 Broad Street. He expanded the colonial house, adding a stair tower with a turret on the east side, and Victorianizing the exterior and interior. Fashionable in its day, the building was again remodeled to its current Colonial Revival style in the 1930s. Courtesy South Caroliniana Library.

A native of Hanover, Germany, Wagener had been a Confederate artillery officer in the Battle of Port Royal in 1861, the years-long defense of Charleston and Sherman's invasion of South Carolina in 1865. After the war he established F.W. Wagener & Company, a wholesale grocery and ship chandlery at 163 East Bay Street. His brother, John Andreas Wagener, was mayor of Charleston, 1871-73.

Backed by Mayor J. Adger Smyth, City Council, subscriptions, and $50,000 from the South Carolina General Assembly, the Charleston Exposition Company was incorporated in 1900. Captain Wagener, its president, donated the use of his Lowndes Grove farm. Wagener was well liked and considered the lifeblood of the South Carolina Inter-State and West Indian Exposition, also called "The West Indian Exposition" or "The Charleston Exposition." With Wagener's land, the Washington Race Course, and other tracts, the exposition had 250 acres less than two miles north of Broad Street.

Bradford Lee Gilbert, a New York architect who had designed the Cotton States Exposition in Atlanta, was hired. Designed in the Spanish Renaissance style, Gilbert's buildings were made of wood that was plastered and painted a creamy off-white. The complex was dubbed the "Ivory City." More than three million feet of lumber went into constructing buildings, which were designed to last only for the duration of the exhibition.

The complex included sunken gardens and walkways lined with roses, azaleas, rhododendrons, camellias, and oleanders. The focal point was the Cotton Palace, 320 feet long with a 75-foot dome. There was a separate Negro Department building, and The Woman's Building was nearby in the Lowndes Grove house, overlooking the Ashley River.

Twenty-two U.S. states and territories, the cities of Cincinnati and Philadelphia, and the republics of Cuba, Honduras, and Guatemala participated. Philadelphia featured the Liberty Bell in its exhibit. Gondolas provided rides on Lake Juanita. There was a zoo and a 6,000-seat auditorium. The midway had a carnival with thrill rides, a 400-foot painting of the Battle of Manassas, a Turkish Parlor featuring imported cigars, a house of horrors, restaurants, and an Eskimo Village. There were camel and elephant rides and a miniature railway.

The Exposition opened December 1, 1901 amid much fanfare. Mayor J. Adger Smyth read a congratulatory message from President Theodore Roosevelt, the band played "My Country 'tis of Thee" and the local German Artillery fired a forty-five-gun salute.

President Roosevelt visited April 2, 1902, accompanied by First Lady Edith Roosevelt. The president reviewed a military parade and addressed an assembly of dignitaries while in Charleston.

The Exposition attracted about 675,000 ticketholders, significantly less than the anticipated million-plus visitors. A severe drought the summer before ruined crops across the Southeast and many

President and Mrs. Roosevelt at the Exposition. Courtesy Library of Congress.

could not afford it. In addition, Charleston experienced one of its worst winters in history.

The Exposition was scheduled to end on June 20, but closed May 3 and was placed into receivership. Yet the event accomplished some of its goals, including an increase in trade with Caribbean interests and establishment of a United Fruit Company branch in Charleston. In addition, the American Tobacco Company opened a cigar factory that provided jobs for locals until the 1970s. The expo also added to Charleston's reputation as a popular tourist destination.

Captain Wagener's memory is preserved through his handsome commercial building on East Bay Street and Wagener Terrace subdivision which was built on his Lowndes Grove property.

F.W. Wagener & Company's wholesale grocery and ship chandlery at 163 East Bay Street. Courtesy The Charleston Museum.

Charleston Germans

Charleston Germans formed a discrete minority, nearly twenty percent of the population, who kept their Teutonic language at home, in their churches (Lutheran and Catholic, mein Gott), civic groups (Freundschaftsbund and German Rifle Club), and the German School. There were the *Deutsche Zeitung* and other newspapers, the Germania Brewery and even the Germania Bank at 34 Broad Street. They were a prosperous group who socially kept aloof from the traditional Charleston elite, and politically formed a powerful bloc. The German Fusiliers and German Artillery saw Confederate service. German families (Tiedeman, Klinck, Merkhardt and Lutjen) built houses in the west end of Broad Street after the Civil War. Their descendants became more Americanized in the early twentieth century.

The Skyscraper Controversy

Towering above Broad Street is the People's Building. At the time of its construction, many hailed it as a sign of progress while others were afraid it would ruin the city's iconic skyline.

The People's Building, 18 Broad Street. Courtesy Library of Congress.

The project was organized by R. Goodwyn Rhett, fiftieth mayor of Charleston and president of the People's National Bank of Charleston, which opened in 1865 and was the oldest national bank in the city. Rhett organized a group of fifty local leaders who amassed $150,000 in contributions and obtained a mortgage for the same amount from New York backers. The building was designed by Swedish architect Victor Frohling of Thompson & Frohling, New York, and built by Simons-Mayrant of Charleston and Hadden Construction Company.

Broad Street looking east before the demolition of the Bank of the State of South Carolina at 18 Broad Street (building with portico on the north side of the street). Courtesy Library of Congress.

Watching construction became a popular spectacle for residents who followed its progress in the local paper. The building opened in April 1911, and many visited just to ride the steel-frame elevators located just beyond the marble-walled foyer.

Done in the Renaissance Revival style, the first two exterior floors were faced with Winnsboro granite, while the upper floors were faced with buff-colored brick and terra cotta. Made of concrete and steel, the building was rated as fireproof and featured steam heat. Inside, the foyer and bank were adorned with classical details and polished marble walls. The bank had a separate entrance at the corner of State Street. Each of the seven floors above had thirteen rooms.

Goody Rhett

Mayor Goodwyn Rhett was a Charleston aristocrat who took full advantage of the prerogatives he inherited. The name

Goodwyn was after his mother, Martha Goodwyn, but friends called him "Goody."

He attended The Porter Academy (later known as Porter Military Academy), Episcopal High School in Virginia, graduated from the University of Virginia in 1883, and then earned a law degree from there. In 1886 he formed the business partnership Trenholm and Rhett, with George M. Trenholm.

R. Goodwyn Rhett, Courtesy Library of Congress.

Rhett entered politics in 1895 as a city alderman and was elected mayor in 1903. His administration was responsible for the establishment of the Board of Public Works and construction of new police and fire stations. He played an instrumental role in the building of Roper Hospital, Union Station, and the Julian Mitchell School, as well as the development of North Charleston. Murray Boulevard was his brainchild as was the development of the exclusive Yeaman's

Hall neighborhood and golf course. Rhett served as president of the Chamber of Commerce of the United States (1916-1918) and chairman of the South Carolina Highway Commission (1920-1926).

Tall, handsome, and urbane, Rhett entertained lavishly and loved to dance and sing. He and President William Howard Taft were lifelong friends. Taft came to see him twice, and the visits are enshrined in Charleston folklore. Taft was a large man, too big for a normal tub, so he brought his bathtub with him. More importantly, when preparing for a dinner party, Rhett is said to have told his butler, William Deas, to "spice up" the crab soup for the President." Deas added some roe, creating that Charleston delicacy, she crab soup.

Rhett took Taft to see the People's Building, treating him to the view from the rooftop. When told that preservationists had expressed concern that the tall new building would adversely affect Charleston's historic skyline, Taft mused that "the view from here is worth it." Taft thus inadvertently provided a promotional catchphrase for future developers, for whom "the view" became a standard selling point.

In 1932, the People's Bank failed while Rhett was in Canada. According to family tradition, Rhett was not given time to save it, and his family lost everything because of a "triple indemnity" penalty, which meant stockholders owed three times what they held in stock. The City of Charleston's payroll funds were in the Peoples Bank and were lost.

Rhett sold assets to satisfy his debts. He and his wife moved from the John Rutledge House on Broad Street and lived in the much smaller Pirate House on Church Street until his death in 1939.

The People's Bank closed in 1936, and the building was purchased by the Southeastern Securities Company. Its president, Charles L. Mullaly, installed two white Italian marble leopards at the main entrance. Carved by an unknown 18th-century artist, the

Broad Street looking west before the Marcus Building fire destroyed buildings on the north side of the street. Courtesy Library of Congress.

lions came from an estate near Boston. In June 2011 the leopard on the right of the entrance was destroyed by vandals. The remaining statue was moved indoors, and replacements were created by Kevin McLean, a College of Charleston art student.

Charleston's first skyscraper is still making history. On August 21, 2017, the rooftop condominium was the site of ABC Television News' Charleston coverage of the total solar eclipse.

Contentious Catholic Mayor Grace

All four of Charleston Mayor John P. Grace's grandparents were Irish immigrants. His grandfather Patrick Grace arrived from County Tipperary in 1833 and became successful enough as a rice mill foreman to send his son James J. Grace to the College of Charleston. Patrick Grace, a first lieutenant in the Irish Volunteers, died defending Charleston in 1863. James Grace became a bookkeeper and married Elizabeth Daly of Charleston. They had ten children: six boys and four girls. John Patrick Grace was born December 30, 1874. The family resided at 10 Society Street in a section of town known as "the Borough."

Life was hard after his father died in 1882. According to biographer Doyle W. Boggs, Mayor Grace liked to tell Horatio Alger stories about his youth. His mother had a small dairy business and young Grace rose before dawn to peddle the milk in a wagon. On slow mornings he parked the wagon under a street light to study his school books. As a youth he attended Catholic school. While attending the High School of Charleston, he worked as an office boy at F.W. Wagener & Co., wholesale grocers.

Grace worked for his uncle, a cotton broker in Greenville, before going to New York in 1888 to work as a steamship clerk. While there, Grace attended debates between labor leaders and theorists at Cooper Union Hall. He sold encyclopedias in Indiana, Ohio and Michigan, all the while absorbing various theories of social reform. In 1899, at the age of twenty-five, Grace returned to conservative Charleston armed with new progressive ideas.

Grace became a bookkeeper and studied law on his own. He caught the attention of U.S. Representative William Elliott, a former Confederate colonel, who hired him as his personal secretary in his Washington office. He enrolled in law school at Georgetown University, graduating in 1902. He returned to Charleston to assist in Elliott's unsuccessful Senate election campaign. In Charleston, he became a law partner of future Congressman W. Turner Logan. In the next thirty years, their Broad Street firm became one of South Carolina's most successful.

Democratic Party Politics

In those days the Democratic Party ruled South Carolina and winning the primary was tantamount to being elected. An Irish Catholic in a Protestant community, Grace did not enjoy the social privileges or political advantages available to local elites popularly known as the Bourbons, or "Boni." Grace abhorred slavery, which he called "the worst form of avarice since it put gold above even human lives and liberty." He blamed the Bourbons for rash acts — Secession and Civil War — to ensure a continuance of the lifestyle of the privileged few. His attitude on race was progressive for the time. He bravely took on cases involving the civil rights of black individuals. In 1907 he won the case of two black men charged with violating the state's peonage statute, the S.C. Farm Labor Law. Not only did Federal Judge H.W. Brawley rule for the defendants, but he also declared the peonage law unconstitutional.

Grace became embroiled in Charleston politics. Being a Progressive Democrat of the activist stripe known as the "Warriors" pitted him against more conservative Democrats in Charleston's two main factions: the aristocratic Broad Street Ring, led by Mayor R. Goodwyn Rhett, a moderate Progressive, and the smaller Tillmanite faction led by Charleston County Sheriff J. Elmore Martin. In 1902, Grace had an unsuccessful bid for the state Senate. In 1904, he lost the primary for county sheriff to Martin. In 1908, he finished last in a crowded race for the U.S. Senate.

The political tide turned in 1911 when Grace ran for mayor of Charleston against businessman Tristram T. Hyde. Hyde was supported by Rhett's Broad Street Ring and Martin's Tillmanite faction. Grace, supported by a coalition of Irish, German and labor voters, won the race by a slim margin. It was known as the "Revolution of 1911." Grace was the first Roman Catholic mayor of Charleston, and the first of several politicians jokingly referred to as the "Catholic Mafia."

Grace hated the British and championed a free Ireland. In 1916 he established the *Charleston American* newspaper as his political voice. After the United States, under President Woodrow Wilson, entered World War I in 1917, Grace's editorials became so anti-Wilson and pro-German that, under the Espionage Act, the American's third-class mailing privilege was suspended. In a compromise with the U.S. Government, Grace resigned as editor to save the newspaper.

The attitudes of the Charleston elite fueled his dislike of Anglophiles. This was not without some basis. When Grace was elected in 1911, outgoing Mayor R. Goodwyn Rhett decided to forgo the ceremonial passing of the keys to City Hall and instead had them delivered to the newly elected mayor by the building's janitor. Grace was outraged, calling it an insult to the citizens of Charleston.

Grace's campaigns were hard fought, and three of his four mayoral primary elections were the most violent in Charleston history. In 1915, 1919, and 1923, the governor sent state militia to police the Charleston polls. In the recount of the 1915 primary, shots rang out in a ward favorable to Grace, and the *Evening Post* newspaper's reporter, Sidney Cohen, was accidently killed. During the confusion, Grace ballots were thrown out of a window of the American Hotel, where the votes were counted. When the dust settled, Hyde won by eighteen votes.

But Hyde lost to Grace when he ran for re-election in 1919. Although the outcome showed Hyde with a one-vote lead, after challenges, the Democratic Executive Committee declared Grace the winner. Four years later, Grace lost to the charismatic young champion of the Charleston elite, Thomas Porcher Stoney. It was Grace's final mayoral campaign.

While mayor, Grace focused on upgrading the city's living conditions by enacting ordinances to develop a clean water supply and an improved sewage system for Charleston. Livestock were banned in the city limits. Charleston High School and the College of Charleston were made free for all white males. Grace took a laissez-faire attitude towards Charleston's traditional pursuit of pleasure. Residents and visitors continued to frequent blind tigers, drink, and gamble.

Mayor Grace's second administration secured state and federal funding for the World War I Memorial Bridge over the Ashley River. Many city streets were paved with asphalt and the city provided land for construction of the Fort Sumter Hotel. In 1920 Grace established the Port Utilities Commission, which purchased the Cooper River wharves from northern investors and improved shipping operations. The commission was a forerunner of the South Carolina Ports Authority, established in 1948.

Cooper River Bridge

John P. Grace's greatest accomplishment occurred years later when he was president of the Cooper River Bridge Company. Until 1929 a ferry system was the only way for the general public to cross the Cooper River between Charleston and Mount Pleasant. Isle of Palms promoters wanted a bridge to expedite the commute to their beach resort. It took a lot of coordination among the investors, the War Department, the Department of Transportation, the courts, and the state Legislature to bring the venture to fruition. Grace is credited with being the driving force behind its construction.

Designed by famed bridge designer Shortridge Hardesty, the Cooper River Bridge opened on August 8, 1929 as a nationally recognized engineering marvel. It was 2.71 miles long and stood 15 feet higher than the Brooklyn Bridge. At the time, it was the third largest truss-cantilever bridge in the world. Construction was completed under budget and three months ahead of schedule at a final cost of just under $6 million, which would be financed with tolls. The initial tolls, designed to be competitive with the ferry rates, were fifty cents per vehicle and driver and fifteen cents for each passenger. Children under the age of six were free. Empty trucks were charged seventy-five cents, loaded $1.50. Motorcycles were thirty-five cents. The toll house was on the Mount Pleasant side of the bridge.

The Cooper River Bridges. Courtesy Library of Congress.

The opening extravaganza lasted three days and involved the greater Charleston community. Then the stock market crashed less than three months later. Declining revenues and rising debts forced the Cooper River Bridge Company into bankruptcy in 1936. Charleston County purchased the bridge in 1941 and continued to collect tolls. The South Carolina Highway Department bought it in 1945 and ended collection of tolls in 1946. The feisty Irishman died at his 174 Broad Street home in June 1940 and the South Carolina General Assembly named the bridge in his honor three years later.

The two-lane bridge was too narrow for modern traffic and a second span was built in 1966 and named after the highway department's chief engineer and administrator, Silas N. Pearman. Both bridges were replaced with a twin-pier cable bridge in 2005. Named for Arthur Ravenel, Jr., the bridge was built ahead of schedule and under budget.

174 Broad Street, home of Mayor John P. Grace. Photograph by Richard P. Donohoe

Truth is...

William B. (Billy) Regan was Charleston's corporation counsel for twenty-seven years. His legal talents were only outmatched by his lightning quick wit, disarming charm, and talent for telling great tales. One of his best stories is about John P. Grace: When Joseph P. Riley was elected Charleston's second Irish Catholic mayor in 1975, the Catholic Bishop of Charleston delivered a letter written by Grace addressed to "The Next Irish Mayor. It read, "Get the Stoneys." This fanciful anecdote has been incorporated into the city's folklore, and different versions have appeared in print, sometimes presented as fact and alternatively as fiction.

Integrated Streetcars

Passengers in a horse-drawn streetcar rumbling along the rails on Broad Street on October 21, 1912, would have reflected Charleston's ethnic diversity. Streetcars had been racially integrated since 1867 when black Charlestonians had won the right to sit alongside white passengers. The next day, October 22, 1912, a Jim Crow ordinance requiring streetcars to be segregated would be ratified by City Council. The ordinance required black passengers to sit in the very back seats. Exceptions were made for a black individual attending white children (the necessary Charleston nursemaid known as the "Dah") or attending a sick or infirm white passenger. Violators could be charged with disorderly conduct and fined up to $50 or sentenced to up to thirty days in jail.

A very tired horse pulls a streetcar on Broad Street, 1883. Courtesy Special Collections, Addlestone Library, College of Charleston.

The results of the streetcar "sit-ins" of 1867 have been hailed as the first incidence of black activists' gaining integrated seating on public transportation. Another Charleston first.

The "sit-in" activists had been inspired by a rally celebrating black civil rights gains, held at Citadel Square (now Marion Square) on March 26, 1867. The rally, attended by about 2,000 people, mostly black, dispersed about 5 p.m. A small group of black men ignored the streetcar company policy that required them to stand on the cars' platforms, entered a car on Meeting Street, and sat down. The conductor, a Mr. Rivers, at first politely explained company policy, but soon waxed less polite. Police were summoned but the sitters still refused to leave.

It was the first of several such incidents. Some protests turned violent, including one at which eleven individuals were arrested in front of the Guard House at Broad and Meeting streets. Soldiers from the Federal occupation troops had to be called in to quell the riot. One protestor, Mary Bowers, complained to the Freedmen's Bureau assistant commissioner in Charleston, Bvt. Gen. Robert K. Scott, who talked with John S. Riggs, president of the Charleston City Railway Company.

Alarmed by the violence, which reduced revenues, and pressured by Federal authority, the railway company board of directors announced on May 3, 1867, that the streetcars would be open to all passengers, regardless of color. Maj. Gen. Daniel E. Sickles, commander of Federal troops in North and South Carolina, followed up with an order de-segregating all public transport – trains, ferries and ships, as well as streetcars.

Riggs is remembered as a self-made man, conscientious to duty and benevolent to the less fortunate. Born in 1823 at Norfolk, Virginia, he came to Charleston as a boy of ten. He married a Charleston native, Martha Reynolds (Mattie) Leitch, and had several children. As a young man he became a real estate developer. He was an auctioneer, using the public auction grounds on the north side of the Exchange.

In 1861, several Charleston businessmen received a state charter for a streetcar company, with Riggs as president. But the Civil War interrupted progress.

On October 17, 1865, Riggs and his board asked Charleston City Council for permission to lay rails. The street railway was in operation in 1866, initially with limited territory including the Blue Line along Broad Street, the Red Line along Rutledge Street (now Avenue), and the Yellow Line along Meeting Street. The company office was in a handsome building remodeled by architect John Henry Devereux at the northwest corner of Broad and East Bay streets, which burned in 1963.

Charleston streetcars continued to be drawn by horses until 1897. Riggs retired in 1896, and a new entity, the Charleston Street Railway Company, absorbed the Charleston City Railway Company and its competitor, the Enterprise Railway Company, which had been organized in 1870. In 1897, they began using electric trolleys. The company became one of the parent companies of the South Carolina Electric and Gas Company, which replaced the trolleys with buses in the 1930s.

It would have been expensive to remove the streetcar tracks, so the City of Charleston simply had them covered with asphalt. The historic tracks are revealed periodically when street paving repairs are made.

Thomas Ezekiel Miller Returns Lost Artifact

The chapter entitled "The Phrenologist and the Skeptic" describes how Clark Mills become a sculptor while living in a studio on Broad Street. One of his early works was a marble bust of John C. Calhoun which the City of Charleston purchased in 1846.

Thomas E. Miller. Courtesy Office of History and Preservation, Clerk of the United States House of Representatives.

The Mills bust sat out the Civil War in City Hall, and apparently nobody missed it when it disappeared during the Reconstruction era. Imagine City Council's surprise in 1931 when eighty-two-year-old Dr. Thomas Ezekiel Miller contacted them with an amazing story. Miller was well known in Charleston. Of mixed race, he was known for his civil rights advocacy for black Americans.

Miller was born in Ferrebeeville, South Carolina, in 1849. His lineage is a matter of conjecture. Eric Bargeron, a graduate student at the University of South Carolina, researched his origins and concluded that Proctor Screven was Miller's father and owner, and Mary Bird, a slave, was his mother. Screven was stabbed to death in 1850, and Mary Bird died a few years later, so Thomas was adopted by the Miller family. Procter Screven was a cousin by marriage of the Heywards. This contradicts historians Eric Foner and Stephen Middleton who wrote that Miller's mother was a fair-skinned, mixed-race daughter of Judge Thomas Heyward, Jr.

The adoptive parents, Richard and Mary Ferrebee Miller, were "free persons of color." The Miller family moved to Charleston in 1851 and Thomas attended schools for free black children. After his mother died, the youth supported himself by selling *Mercury* newspapers at hotels.

During the war he delivered newspapers on the Charleston & Savannah Railroad. When the Confederate Army seized the railroads, he was conscripted as a conductor. Miller went north with the N.Y. 24th Negro Regiment to Harts Island, New York and from there to Hudson College where he finished his education and earned a scholarship to Lincoln University in Chester County, Pennsylvania.

Miller returned to South Carolina and won his first elective office as a school commissioner in Beaufort. He went on to study law at the newly integrated University of South Carolina and was admitted to the bar in 1875.

Armed with a law degree, Miller returned to Beaufort and became a prominent member of the Republican Party. He was elected to the state House of Representatives and served one year before entering the congressional race for the seat of Robert Smalls, the slave who had become a Northern hero when he escaped Confederate Charleston on the *Planter* during the war.

Miller lost to the Democratic candidate and contested the election. Through a lot of political machinations, he was finally seated near the end of his term. According to the 1891 Congressional Record, Miller supported the Federal Elections Bill and chastised his congressional colleagues about the deterioration of civil rights in the South.

Although Miller failed to be re-elected to the 52nd Congress, he was elected to the state House of Representatives for a single term in 1894 and was a delegate to the 1895 state constitutional convention. He and five other black Republicans refused to sign the Tillmanite constitution which restricted black voting rights.

Ironically, it was in education that Miller left his mark on South Carolina. In exchange for promising to leave politics, Miller helped establish the State Negro College (now South Carolina State University). He remained president of the college until 1911 when he was forced to resign by Gov. Coleman L. Blease, who did not believe in the education of blacks.

Entry gate to South Carolina State College, which T.E. Miller helped establish. Courtesy South Carolina State University.

Miller retired to Charleston and supported American entry into World War I, helping recruit more than 30,000 black soldiers. In 1923, the Miller family moved to Philadelphia.

While in the north, Miller saw Clark Mills' Calhoun bust in Washington, D.C., in the office of Charleston-born attorney Archibald Grimké. A son of Henry Grimké and his enslaved servant Nancy Weston, Archibald Grimké was a nephew of the famous abolitionists, Sarah and Angelina Grimké. He attended a school started by Gilbert Pillsbury, a Freedman's Bureau official. After serving as Reconstruction mayor of Charleston, Pillsbury took Calhoun's bust to Washington. Grimké practiced law with Pillsbury. In a curious twist of fate, when Pillsbury died, Clark Mills' marble bust passed to Archibald Grimké.

The April 28, 1931, minutes of the Charleston City Council finish the narrative: "Desirous of restoring the relic to the people of Charleston, Grimké had requested him to return it [the bust] to his native city, and Dr. Miller stated that in response to his promise and his responsibility, he was now discharging that trust. There were no strings...or any considerations involved, other than his desire to bring to his people one of their treasures."

Miller returned to Charleston in 1934 and died in 1938. His obituary in the Journal of Negro History described him as "one of the most useful men of his time." His legacy was inscribed on his tombstone in the Brotherly Association Cemetery in Charleston: "I served God and all the people, loving the white man not less, but the Negro needed me most."

Today the bust is again in its intended home, displayed beside the portrait of John C. Calhoun in the anteroom off City Council Chambers.

The Boy Soldier and the Jazzman Mayor

The boyhood home of Charleston Mayor John Tecklenburg at 130 Broad Street was built in 1881-82 by the so-called "Boy Soldier of the Confederacy" — John Carsten Tiedeman.

The site at the corner of Broad and Friend (now Legare) streets was deeded to Tiedeman by his father Otto Tiedeman Sr. on July 19, 1881. The lot had been part of a larger piece of property acquired by Otto Sr. from the estate of Josiah S. Payne, whose slave auction house was at 32-34 Broad Street.

130 Broad Street. Photograph by Richard P. Donohoe.

The residence and other buildings on the lot had been destroyed in the Great Fire of 1861, and the lot was still vacant in 1881. Otto Sr. divided the large lot and conveyed the corner portion to his son John and a lot facing Friend Street to son Otto Jr.

John C. Tiedeman built a house that reflects the popularity of the Italian Villa style, first appearing in Charleston in the 1840s. Elements of the style include a prominent bay window and over-hanging bracketed cornices; updated with pendants on the brackets, an element of the Queen Anne style that was just becoming popular in the city. Otherwise, the house design is conservative, including the classical square columns of the piazzas, and the side-hall plan that gives the house a rectangular footprint. The interior is distinguished by ceiling and wall frescoes by skilled Charleston artists, typical of the time.

John C. Tiedeman was barely eighteen years of age when Union Gen. William Tecumseh Sherman entered South Carolina from Savannah with a huge army in December 1864. Private Tiedeman served in the South Carolina Battalion of State Cadets, composed of young men from the South Carolina Military Academy (now The Citadel) in Charleston and the Arsenal Military Academy in Columbia.

Tiedeman, a Citadel cadet, was with a Confederate battalion at the Battle of Tulifinny, December 6-9, 1864. The battalion formed one-third of the Confederate force of 900 sent to oppose a Union force of about 5,000 men entrenched on DeVeaux's Neck at the confluence of the Tulifinny and Coosawhatchie rivers in what is now Jasper County. The cadets were assigned to guard a strategic trestle where the Charleston and Savannah Railroad crossed the Tulifinny River. When Union soldiers advanced close to the bridge, the cadets mounted a surprise attack that drove them back. Two days later the cadets repulsed a Union assault on the bridge.

The cadets were acclaimed for their tenacity and valor during these engagements. Afterwards, Tiedeman and other cadets were assigned to duty on James Island. Recounting this experience, Tiedeman's 1938 obituary in *The News and Courier* was headlined, "Boy Soldier of Confederacy."

Mural of The Battle of Tulifinny by David Humphreys Miller, Daniel Library. Courtesy The Citadel.

Tiedeman later joined his father Otto, a native of Germany, in the wholesale grocery business. Eventually, he became president of Otto Tiedeman & Sons at East Bay Street and Accommodation Wharf. The firm was one of Charleston's major dealers in sugar and supplied grocery stores in Charleston and other parts of the state. Tiedeman served on Charleston City Council, including the Ways and Means Committee. He was a director of the First National Bank.

Tiedeman first married Caroline Louise Probst, who died in 1912. His second marriage was to his next-door neighbor, Mary Elizabeth Klinck. She died in 1930, after having served for many years on the City Board of Parks and Playgrounds.

Tiedeman died in 1938, bequeathing the family home to his daughter, Louise Tiedeman Hartley. In 1946, she conveyed the property to the Trustees of Trinity Methodist Church. For the next decade 130 Broad Street was used as a parsonage.

The Tecklenburgs

Henry Christian John Tecklenburg Jr., whose ancestors had come to Charleston from Germany before the Civil War, bought the house in 1958. Known as "Teck," the Clemson University graduate was in the real estate and insurance business. He was appointed as Charleston County auditor in 1957. In 1963 he entered the oil business, serving as chairman of the board of the Power Oil Company in Orangeburg, president of Estec Petroleum Company in Charleston, and chairman of the board of Southern Oil. He served on the board of the S.C. State Ports Authority, of which he was chairman, 1982-1985. When he died in 1993, President Bill Clinton had just appointed him undersecretary of travel and tourism in the U.S. Department of Commerce.

Henry Tecklenburg Jr. married Esther Hynes Herlihy in 1950. She came from an oil company family in Orangeburg. She served on City Council, 1980-1986, and as mayor pro tempore in 1981. Their son John J. Tecklenburg (one of five children) is currently mayor of Charleston. A graduate of Georgetown University who attended Berklee College of Music in Boston, Tecklenburg was a commercial realtor and is an accomplished jazz musician. He was the city's director of economic development from 1995 to 1999. He was elected mayor of Charleston in 2015, and re-elected in 2019.

Mayor John Tecklenburg. Courtesy City of Charleston.

Porgy

O ne of the most picturesque institutions of old Charleston was street vendors hawking their wares. Some sold ice for "ice boxes," while others sold vegetables, flowers, fish, shrimp, oysters, handmade baskets, and more.

Street Vendor — Elizabeth O'Neill Verner
— Courtesy M. M. R. Eastman.

Many women vendors carried their wares in baskets balanced on top of their heads. Men pushed weather-beaten, makeshift carts decorated with chips of paint that somehow clung to the boards. Two large wheels at the back of the cart rolled it along; the front had a vertical board to keep the cart from tipping over. Carts were used by shrimp and fish men, vegetable men, and a peanut man who roamed the streets, chanting their familiar refrains. Their mellifluous voices were a beloved sound.

Charleston's most famous street vendor is the fictional Porgy, an endearing character made famous by DuBose Heyward in his best-selling novel about a crippled street-beggar living in "Catfish Row." As with most Charleston history, Porgy is intimately connected to Broad Street and its environs.

The Creator of Porgy

DuBose Heyward was a descendant of Judge Thomas Heyward Jr., a signer of the Declaration of Independence. As a youth, DuBose was often ill and dropped out of high school at age fourteen. He contracted polio at eighteen and typhoid fever at twenty. While convalescing, he passed the time writing verses and stories.

Thomas Heyward, Jr., oil by Margaret Miller after copy of Stolle's copy of Jeremiah Theus. Courtesy The Charleston Museum.

His mother, Jane Screven DuBose Heyward, a poet and story-teller, influenced his interest in Gullah culture and he became a keen observer of African American life. He grew up on Church Street not far from crowded tenements known as Cabbage Row, and was inspired by the colorful exploits of black men, women and children. His social conscience was derived from his exposure to African American men on the wharves where he worked as a cotton checker.

Heyward became a major figure in the Charleston Renaissance. His literary career began with a one-act play locally produced in 1913. He, Hervey Allen, and others founded the Poetry Society of South Carolina in 1920. Heyward edited the society's yearbooks and earned a "Contemporary Verse" award in 1921. In 1922 he and Allen published *Carolina Chansons: Legends of the Low Country*. The same year Heyward married Dorothy Kuhns, whom he met at the MacDowell (art) Colony in Peterborough, New Hampshire. Heyward operated a successful insurance and real estate company at 87 Broad Street, achieving enough financial independence to leave business and devote his time to literature.

Heyward was one of the first white authors who brought alive members of the black community through his writing. He

African American men toting rice on a wharf. Courtesy Library of Congress.

85-87 Broad Street c. 1945. Courtesy Library of Contress.

published *Jasbo Brown and Other Poems* in 1924, and supplemented his income by lecturing. After *Porgy* became a bestseller, his
wife Dorothy adapted the story into a Broadway play that ran
for 367 performances.

Composer George Gershwin and Heyward collaborated on an
operatic version of *Porgy* while staying in a Folly Beach house in the
summer of 1934. They went to black churches so Gershwin could
get a sense of Gullah music and culture. Meanwhile in New York,
George's brother Ira wrote lyrics to some of the opera's songs, most
notably, "It Ain't Necessarily So." The libretto and most of the
lyrics, including "Summertime," were written by Heyward.

DuBose Heyward died from a heart attack in Tryon, North
Carolina at the age of fifty-four. He is buried in St. Philip's western churchyard near the tomb of John C. Calhoun.

America's First Folk Opera

Porgy and Bess helped make Charleston even more famous. It was the first American opera performed on Broadway with an integrated cast. Although Washington, D. C. was still segregated, when the production went on tour, the singers made history by demanding that the audience be integrated. It was not a box office success when it was first produced and met with mixed emotions in the African American community until Leontyne Price played the role of Bess in the 1950s.

Scene from *Porgy and Bess*, 1935-1936, Theater Guild. Courtesy Library of Congress.

The first Charleston production was performed at the Gaillard Auditorium in 1970 and again in 1993. In 2012, on the seventy-fifth anniversary of George Gershwin's death, the Footlight Players secured the right to perform the opera at the Dock Street Theatre. Typically, copyright owners grant performance rights only to venues that can seat more than 1,000; however, they made an exception to the smaller seating capacity because of the opera's ties to Charleston.

Leontyne Price in *Porgy & Bess.* Courtesy Library of Congress.

The Real Porgy

Heyward's Porgy was based on a real person, Samuel Smalls, a street vendor who roamed around town in a goat cart. He sold peanut cakes to college students at the corner of King and George streets, and he parked his goat cart on Broad Street to panhandle tourists.

Smalls was a regular sight on the Cooper River wharves where he kept company with Mosquito Fleet fishermen who went out in small wooden boats, some with sails, at dawn every morning. He was popular with the fishermen because his upper torso development made him a good oarsman and enabled him to haul in nets. They nicknamed him "Porgy" after the fish caught off the barrier islands.

Like the fictional Porgy, Smalls was said to be quite a ladies' man. Smalls was charged with murder in a disagreement over the affections of a woman, and was jailed on Magazine Street until some businessmen got him released. Heyward learned of Smalls through a *News and Courier* article about his arrest after a merry chase down several alleys.

After the opera, Porgy became famous. People wanted to know more about Sammy Smalls, but it was too late. Even knowledgeable old-timers could not positively identify which downtown tenement he called home. According to the family who operated a business at 51 Broad Street, he usually parked his cart in the alley behind the building.

Samuel Smalls died in 1924 and was buried in the churchyard at James Island Presbyterian Church. In 1986, a marker was erected at his gravesite. Memories of Porgy and his goat cart lingered on long past his death when Gordon Langley Hall opened an antique store on St. Michael's Alley just behind Nos. 51-53 Broad Street. Its name? The Goat Cart, of course.

Charleston street vendors. They are posed under a cantilevered balcony, known in Charleston as a "run", usually attached to outbuildings. Courtesy Library of Congress.

Saving the College of Charleston

L ucius Mendel Rivers was born in Berkeley County and attended the College of Charleston and the South Carolina School of Law. After passing the bar in 1932, he established a law practice and served in the state House of Representatives, 1934-36. Rivers served in the U.S. House of Representatives, from 1941 until his death in 1970.

Mendel Rivers speaking at a Veterans Day freedom rally at the Washington Monument, in front of the America flag, gesturing with the V sign for victory. Courtesy Library of Congress.

Congressman Rivers represented mostly farming counties and wanted to be on the Agriculture Committee. But that committee was full, so he was appointed to the Naval Affairs Committee. Deeply disappointed, he complained to any who would listen until a colleague reminded him that there was a Navy base and shipyard in his district and war was imminent. Rivers took the hint, and the rest is history.

During his years in Washington, Rivers brought thousands of military jobs to the Charleston area. The Charleston Navy Shipyard expanded into a major U.S. naval base and a former Army airfield became Charleston Air Force Base. With the establishment of the Naval Weapons Station, Charleston was the nation's major Polaris missile submarine port. Other facilities included the Atlantic Mine Fleet Headquarters and its Mine Warfare School.

The federal government became the largest single employer in the Charleston area at that time. In 1969 military bases contributed $317 million to the local economy, amounting to 55 percent of the region's total payroll. Military expansion also lured numerous private defense contractors to the area.

Rivers promoted a strong U.S. military to counter the influence of the Soviet Union during the Cold War. He was known as the "Serviceman's Best Friend" because he sponsored many improvements in pay, medical care, and other benefits for military personnel.

When he died, flags flew at half-staff at military bases all over the world. The Navy commissioned the USS *L. Mendel Rivers* (SSN-686) soon after his death, making him one of few South Carolinians so honored. Others are the "Swamp Fox," Francis Marion; the first commandant of the U. S. Marine Corps, Charleston native William Ward Burrows; Naval hero in Tripoli during the Barbary War, Lieutenant Ralph Delancy Izard; Vice President and U. S. Senator John C. Calhoun; sculptor of the equestrian statue of Andrew Jackson near the White House, Clark Mills; Governor Benjamin Ryan Tillman, who was instrumental in getting the Naval Base established in 1901; and PFC Ralph Henry Johnson, the Marine who posthumously received the Congressional Medal of Honor for his unselfish heroism in Vietnam.

Posthumous recognition for Rivers includes a monument with his bust in the garden of the O.T. Wallace County Office Building on Meeting Street, the Rivers bust first placed on Rivers Avenue and relocated to Riverfront Park in North Charleston. On D-Day 2021, the same date Chairman Rivers had selected for the inaugural flight of the C 5A Galaxy into Charleston Air Force Base, a historical marker was unveiled on Charlotte Street in Charleston commemorating the L. Mendel Rivers Federal Building, which had been sold to a private investor and renamed.

Contributed by L. Mendel Rivers, Jr.

"Big Joe" Riley

Joseph P. Riley Sr.'s grandparents, Patrick and Ann Collins Riley, were among Irish immigrants who left their homeland after the potato famine and arrived in Charleston in the 1850s. Patrick found a job manufacturing and delivering gas, an industry that came into its own when Charleston started illuminating its streets with gaslight. When the Civil War began, Patrick volunteered for the Confederate Army, but his skills in gas production were considered so important that he remained in Charleston.

"Big Joe" Riley and his family on the steps of their home. "Little Joe", later Mayor of Charleston, is on the right. Courtesy Mayor Joseph P. Riley, Jr.

Patrick's son Andrew grew up during the Reconstruction era. He was elected to City Council, where one of his closest allies was Mayor John P. Grace. Civic minded, Andrew achieved such prominence that when he died, flags at City Hall and every fire station in the city were lowered to half-staff.

Joseph Patrick Riley, the eighth child of Andrew and Mary Emily Oliver Riley, was twelve when his father died. Joe worked for his mother until he attended the University of South Carolina, but the Great Depression brought him home after a year into his studies.

He tried to enter the service when World War II started, but was rejected for poor eyesight. He signed up on a patient transport ship and spent months overseas providing support for Gen. George Patton's ambitious operations. After he returned home, Riley continued in the war effort through the Charleston Servicemen's Center and the Civilian Defense Council and watched for German submarines from lookout posts on the Isle of Palms.

Riley was twenty-five years old when he opened the Joseph Riley Real Estate and Insurance Agency. In January 1943, he purchased 13 Broad Street. This purchase coincided with the birth of his only son and namesake, and from then on, he was known as "Big Joe."

When L. Mendel Rivers ran for Congress in 1940, Joe Riley Sr. was his campaign treasurer, and the second floor of 13 Broad Street, known as 13½ Broad Street, became Rivers' congressional office until the completion of the Federal Building on Meeting Street. According to Brian Hicks' *The Mayor*, Big Joe was "a major player in the county's Democratic Party and ally of Congressman Rivers."

13 Broad Street. Courtesy Library of Congress.

The Famous "Trip to Barnwell"

Joe Riley Sr. was a key player in saving the College of Charleston. In the 1960s, the College failed to comply with racial desegregation required by the Civil Rights Act of 1964. Federal grants for programs were cancelled and students could not get federal loans. Enrollment declined to a few hundred students. In 1967 black students were admitted, and federal funds restored. But the college remained in financial trouble, its endowment having been depleted. By 1969 the College was on the verge of collapse. A new president was sought.

Several alumni and community leaders approached Theodore S. (Ted) Stern, the charismatic commanding officer of the Charleston Naval Supply Center. Nearing retirement, Stern had received several prestigious employment offers and was not interested in the college presidency. That changed when Congressman Rivers, chairman of the House Armed Services Committee, encouraged Stern to accept the College of Charleston job. Stern did and Rivers conveniently fast-tracked his retirement from the Navy.

Speaker Sol Blatt and President Stern. Courtesy College of Charleston Special Collections Library Waddell Collection.

President Stern presiding at a College of Charleston commencement. Courtesy College of Charleston Special Collections Library Waddell Collection.

Stern's appointment occurred soon after the state established the S.C. Commission on Higher Education and determined that the Lowcountry needed a comprehensive state institution of higher learning. The question was whether to create a new university or expand an existing school. The College of Charleston's board of trustees was faced with the dilemma of competing with another institution or allowing a state takeover. They chose the latter, then awaited the legislature's approval.

At that time, the political strongmen who controlled the state legislature were known as the Barnwell Ring. That's because the speaker of the House was Sol Blatt and the president pro tem of the Senate was Edgar Brown, both from Barnwell. But Blatt was a University of South Carolina sports fan and Brown was a Clemson man, and neither wanted another institution competing with their favorite universities.

Stern needed political clout, so he contacted Joe Riley Sr., who enlisted the help of Rivers, and the three took a private plane to Barnwell to get the speaker's support. As Blatt recounted later, "I was unilaterally opposed to the College of Charleston coming into the state system. They drank my liquor, they ate my food and by the time the evening was over, I was the strongest supporter of the College coming in."

After securing Blatt's support, Rivers lobbied legislators and cleverly played Blatt off against the equally powerful Edgar Brown by reminding each of them privately about the important roles their cherished institutions — South Carolina and Clemson — would play in the new state system. By the time the matter came before the legislature, all opposition had been removed, but still, Rivers took no chances. Having once been a legislator himself, he personally attended the voting in Columbia, wrangling a seat on the dais of the House beside Speaker Blatt as the votes were cast. The bill passed unanimously, and Stern went on to assure accreditation and set the trajectory for what the College of Charleston has become today.

Equally important, Congressman Rivers introduced Joe Riley Jr. to politics in action by having him intern one summer in his Washington office. Young Joe was a Citadel cadet at that time. He later opened a law practice at 13 Broad Street, served in the State House of Representatives, 1969-1974, and in 1975 was elected mayor of Charleston, a job he held for forty years. When Mendel Rivers died a few months after securing the college's future, Big Joe Riley wept openly, saying he would never again have such a friend.

Historic Building Saved from Condo Cannibalization

The southwest corner of Broad and East Bay streets has been a prime business location since Charles Town was laid out on the peninsula in the 1670s.

State Bank of South Carolina. Courtesy College of Charleston, Special Collections Library, Waddell Collection.

The Fire of 1740 damaged or destroyed most of the buildings in the neighborhood, including the nearby Half Moon Battery and its gun carriages. Property loss in that fire amounted to £250,000, and for the only time in the colony's history, Parliament came to its aid and sent £20,000 for relief.

The site of 1 Broad Street changed hands numerous times before it was purchased for the State Bank of South Carolina by its president, Edward Sebring. In anticipation of building a banking facility and a commercial building next door, the purchase included the corner lot and adjacent properties. The building was completed in 1853.

Sebring had moved from New York City in 1820 and quickly became a leader in Charleston's business community. Sebring commissioned Jones & Lee, one of Charleston's leading architectural firms, to design buildings on his downtown property. Edward Culliatt Jones was noted for the "Italian villa" style and had designed Trinity Methodist Church on Meeting Street and Roper Hospital on Queen Street as well as public buildings throughout the state. In 1852 he partnered with his former student Francis D. Lee, whose work includes, on Archdale Street, the Unitarian Church's fan tracery vaulting reminiscent of Henry VII's chapel at Westminster, and the Moorish Revival Farmers and Exchange Bank on East Bay Street. The four-year partnership produced additional noteworthy buildings.

After the partnership dissolved in 1857, Lee moved his office from the corner of Broad and Church streets into the bank building at 1 Broad Street.

The State Bank of South Carolina building was designed in the Italian Renaissance Revival style. Its brownstone façade was quarried in Connecticut, and each lion head keystone above the windows is said to have been patterned after one of the bank managers. The entry doors featured solid pine, faux grained to look like Cuban mahogany.

The interior catered to the tastes of Charleston's luxury-loving elite. Above the bank was an open floor with oversized windows facing both streets. Flooded with natural light, this space housed an exclusive subscription-only reading room that was part of the national mercantile library movement dedicated to "shielding young men from the society of the vicious and profane and furthering their moral cultivation by providing an anchor against moral shipwreck on the lee shore of the brothel and grog shop."

The third floor had private office spaces, while cooler accommodations were in a half-basement. The building was on high land enabling the sub-ground-level rooms to enjoy ventilation provided by windows that opened onto a trench over which a grating was installed to protect pedestrians.

According to novelist and historian William Gilmore Simms, "The State Bank is a flourishing institution, though the outsider must not imagine that its name involves any connection with the body politic. ... The finish of the interior is extremely fine — the oak carving being rich and abundant, and the paving of the Banking Hall being of the most showy fashion of encaustic tiling."

Collapse of the Bank

The new bank was the pride of lower Broad Street until the Federal bombardment started in 1863. By the end of the Civil War, the building had been wrecked. The destruction was so severe that it made the April 1, 1865, issue of *Frank Leslie's Illustrated Newspaper*.

Bank interior after the bombardment. Courtesy The Charleston Museum.

The State Bank of South Carolina's fate was equally dramatic. Just before the evacuation of Charleston near the close of the war, Sebring took the bank's negotiable assets and valuable papers to a country house near Camden for safe keeping. But on February 27, 1865, a detachment of Sherman's army passed through the area, found the valuables, and appropriated them.

To make matters worse, the State Bank of South Carolina had 100 pre-war Blue Ridge Railroad Company $1,000 bonds, which the bank's cashier, Benjamin M. Lee, had removed. He was stopped near modern-day Lake City by Yankee troops and relieved of the bonds. With its assets gone, the bank collapsed.

While Sebring was sheltering in Camden, his home in Charleston was ransacked. The showcase mansion on Calhoun Street overlooked Bennett's Mill Pond. Union Gen. Edward E. Potter's men ("Potter's Plunderers") carried off valuables, including the family silver.

In the late 1840s, Sebring had worked with architect Jones on the design of an elegant cemetery north of the city on Magnolia Umbra Plantation, once the country seat of colonial Justice William Burrows. But following the Civil War, Magnolia Cemetery proved to be Sebring's ultimate undoing. A Union soldier was buried in the cemetery, and Confederate veterans were outraged. Sebring, a cemetery trustee, was held responsible for selling the burial plot and sentenced to be hanged, although the order was never carried out. Sebring never regained prominence in the community.

The architects of Sebring's bank fared better. During the war, Jones was attached to the commissary of the South Carolina 1st Regiment of Reserves. After the war, he moved to Memphis, where he had a second career designing landmarks in Tennessee, Mississippi, and elsewhere in the South. Whereas Jones' early buildings were produced with traditional techniques and tools, by 1890 he had mastered steel and rivets, thus enabling him to produce the first skyscraper south of St. Louis, which stands in Memphis today. One of his churches later became Clayborn Temple, where the 1960s civil rights sanitation worker marches started and ended. Martin Luther King spoke there several times. Jones died in Memphis in 1902.

Francis D. Lee was given a commission in the engineer corps and was at Fort Walker during the battle at Port Royal in 1861. He served on Gen. Pierre G. T. Beauregard's staff during the siege of Charleston and planned Battery Wagner on Morris Island. He also invented a Confederate torpedo boat. After the war, Emperor Napoleon III invited him to France to showcase his invention. In 1866, Lee moved to St. Louis, where he formed a partnership with Thomas Annan and designed many buildings, including the Merchant's Exchange and the Jesuit's College. He died in St. Louis in 1885.

Fraser, Trenholm & Associates

After the war, to regain their property and citizenship, former Confederates had to swear allegiance to the Unites States. Officials in the Confederate government fared less well, especially George Alfred Trenholm, the former Confederate secretary of the treasury, who owned 1 Broad Street for a time.

CITIZENS OF CHARLESTON, S.C., TAKING THE OATH OF ALLEGIANCE SOON AFTER THE EVACUATION OF THE CITY BY GENERAL HARDEE

Ex-Confederates taking the Oath of Allegiance. Courtesy Miriam and Ira D. Wallach Division of Art, Prints and Photographs: Picture Collection, The New York Public Library.

Trenholm was sent to Fort Pulaski, Georgia. In October 1865, President Andrew Johnson paroled him and three other prisoners. Still, Trenholm was a man without citizenship.

That fall, the Reverend Dr. A. Toomer Porter of Charleston persuaded Trenholm to ask President Johnson for a pardon. Porter thought that men like Trenholm were essential to the business welfare of the city and state, so he obtained endorsements from occupying Gen. Daniel Sickles and other locals, and traveled to New York City to obtain endorsements from influential Republicans before approaching President Johnson, who pardoned Trenholm on October 15, 1866.

With his citizenship restored, Trenholm reorganized his brokerage under the name George A. Trenholm & Son Company. During the Civil War, Fraser, Trenholm, and Associates was heavily involved in blockade running and kept excellent books, which were confiscated after Charleston fell. Trenholm and his wartime partners were forced to liquidate their real estate holdings when the Federal government sued for import duties on illegal blockade goods.

Trenholm died in December 1876. Because he had been the president of the Chamber of Commerce, all the ships in the harbor flew their flags at half-mast in tribute to his memory.

The Rev. Dr. Porter on George Alfred Trenholm

In business Mr. Trenholm was king. He was the absolute master of local banking and the cotton trade. He had his ships, and his word in Broad Street and on East Bay was law; but it is of the man I would write. He was tall and handsome, graceful in his manners... he had the sweetest smile of any man I ever saw... His alms were not so well known... but I, his pastor, saw what he would not let the world see, and many families that the community knew not of, were made comfortable and lived in ease because of his generosity....

He succeeded Mr. C.G. Menninger as Secretary of the Treasury of the Confederate States. He, along with Mr. Wagner, inaugurated the blockade-running. They brought immense stores, and guns and ammunition into the Confederacy. It is a sad commentary that the generation of today, even in this community [Charleston], have little knowledge of the greatest man who ever lived in it. (1896)

George Walton Williams

One Broad Street was sold in 1875 to the Carolina Savings Bank of Charleston, which operated from that site for eighty-two years. The bank's founder, George Walton Williams, was an entrepreneur with an enormously successful wholesale grocery business.

George Walton Williams in middle age. — From Coulton's *George Walton Williams: The Life of a Southern Merchant and Banker, 1820-1907.*

At the onset of the Civil War, the General Assembly appointed Williams commissary to procure food for soldiers' families, and the city appointed him manager of the subsistence stores to procure food for the poor of Charleston. He was also a city alderman and chairman of the Committee of Ways and Means. Through his powerful connections, he procured the needed supplies and did not charge a cent for his services. Thus, thousands of suffering and destitute residents were provided food and supplies until the end of the war.

Williams was later one of the emissaries sent by Mayor Charles Macbeth to negotiate an orderly surrender of Charleston to Federal forces. Williams' quick actions saved the Confederate commissary from destruction, and on the day the city fell, thousands of people were fed amid the confusion.

"Feeding 8,000 people with rations of rice and salt at West Point Mills, on the Ashley River, Charleston S.C. — From a sketch by our Special Artist, W.T. Crane, April 15, 1865." *Harper's Weekly.*

During the war, Williams' profits from blockade running are estimated to have been more than one million dollars, which he invested in British sterling instead of Confederate currency. After the war, his wholesale grocery business was the first to resume business in Charleston. In 1865 he chartered the Banking House of George Walton Williams. In 1875 he moved the bank to 1 Broad Street.

Three years after Alexander Graham Bell patented the telephone, the second floor of 1 Broad housed the first telephone exchange in South Carolina. From 1877 until 1897 the third floor was used as the local office of the U.S. Signal Corps, and by its successor, the U.S. Weather Bureau.

Like Trenholm, Williams contributed much to the betterment of the devastated economy. But Williams is best remembered for his residence at 16 Meeting Street, which is considered one of the most important Victorian mansions on the Eastern Seaboard.

After the Earthquake of 1886, the Signal Corps oversaw 1 Broad Street's damage mitigation. A spider web of earthquake rods was placed above the building's original roof line, and a new roof was installed above the rods. The original cornice of the building fell during the quake, and a cast iron replacement cornice served as the anchor for the rods. The building was further stabilized with earthquake rods disguised as a new row of small, decorative lion heads. After the 1938 tornado swept through Broad Street, another set of quake rods was added to the third floor.

Three layers of stabilizing iron rods were discovered during a recent restoration. Structural engineer Mark Dillion said, "The tension rod system in 1 Broad is the most elegant and comprehensive of any system I have seen in my thirty-two-year career, and the roof rod design closely approximates what modern earthquake engineering design is supposed to do."

One Broad Street has been renovated several times. In 1948 the Carolina Savings Bank updated the building and the architectural firm of Simons and Lapham designed its mid-century look. Since it never flooded, the basement became a storage area.

In 1978 Bankers Trust carried out a $320,000 restoration. Ball Corporation developed a brownstone polymer coating to stabilize the surface and made repairs. A lush interior was designed by John Ragsdale and included a major commission by Charleston blacksmith Philip Simmons to create ornate, iron teller grills and extensive stair and landing railings. Irish artist Jim McDonald (known for his paintings of the *Titanic* and shipyards) was commissioned to recreate the hand-painted ceiling of the president's office.

Another owner, Broad Street Ventures, stripped the interior in anticipation of converting to luxury condominiums, but the recession of 2007 stopped the work. It was subsequently purchased by Mark Beck, an entrepreneur and founder of a multinational technology firm based in Mooresville, North Carolina.

Beck and his team returned the interior to its 1853 design, thus sparing the building from being chopped into multiple apartments. In January 2020, the 1 Broad Street renovation received the Carolopolis Award from the Preservation Society of Charleston.

A never-circulated 1861 printer's proof for the State Bank of South Carolina's $5 note features a picture of the building. Owner Mark Beck commissioned an acrylic artwork for the building's Broad Street entrance. Courtesy Mark Beck.

Walker, Evans & Cogswell

In 1854, 3 Broad Street was constructed for Edward Sebring. Like the bank next door, it was designed by architects Jones & Lee. The façade featured Charleston grey brick laid in Flemish bond, with brownstone cornices and sills on the upper-level windows. The building lost the brownstone cornice in the 1886 Earthquake. Its replacement was made of pressed tin.

The first occupants of 3 Broad Street were Samuel G. Courtenay, bookseller, on the first floor and publishers Walker & James on the floors above. When the Walker, Evans & Cogswell Company purchased the building, a fourth floor was added, and the rear was joined with their East Bay book binding operation.

Walker, Evans & Cogswell Company was considered Charleston's best printer, engraver and lithographer. It was founded in 1821 when John C. Walker opened a stationery and book binding business at 15 Broad Street. When his brothers joined the business, the bookbinding business moved around the corner to 111 East Bay Street.

The company was retained as the daily printer for the Secession Convention, and later lithographed the state's Ordinance of Secession. John Walker became a silent partner in 1860, and the company name was changed to Evans & Cogswell, Confederate Government Printers and Lithographers. During the war, they printed small-denomination paper currency, government bonds, stock certificates, stamps, the *Soldier's Prayer Book*, and books on war tactics and medicine for the Confederacy.

When Union artillery shells from Morris Island began to reach the lower city, the State Bank of South Carolina was hit. The Confederate government then relocated the printing operation to Columbia, where operations continued until Sherman's troops arrived February 1865 and burned the printing plant. The company then returned to Charleston and resumed operations under its original name.

In 1909, a new printing plant called the Cogswell Building was built next door to the East Bay retail shop. At that time the first two stories of 3 Broad Street became retail space and offices, while the upper floors were used for storage.

The business closed in 1982, and 3 Broad Street was renovated with office condominiums on the upper floors and a retail space on the ground floor. The Cogswell Building on East Bay was converted into residential condominiums.

3 Broad Street. Courtesy Library of Congress.

Mysterious Paintings

The 20th century brought an increase in tourism and real estate sales through advertising promotions that included enticing legends and other fanciful misinformation. Such is the case with 54 Broad Street.

54 Broad Street. Courtesy Library of Congress.

In 1930 an intriguing article about the re-emergence of so-called ancient paintings inside a small dependency behind the main house at the address appeared in *The News and Courier*. Six years later, the mysterious paintings were mentioned in again in another article. Indeed, what appeared to be primitive paintings had slowly appeared on some walls in the dependency.

It seems that sometime earlier that century, the dependency's basement was whitewashed, and as time and moisture caused the wash to flake, strange images came to light. Artist Reginald B. Abbott-Smith was using the building, 54½ Broad, for a studio, saw what was happening and painstakingly began to remove the whitewash. He uncovered a trove of eerie pictures in the semi-darkness of the basement. One was a likeness of Napoleon sitting by a table. Another seemed to be a battle scene at Waterloo. Another of a dog was framed in gold paint.

The artwork apparently had been created by projecting a picture on the wall with a projecting lantern, and someone outlined the images in black before painting within the lines. Although old timers remembered seeing the murals before the turn of the century, no one knew who painted them. Beyond oral tradition, the only clue was, according to old city directories, Captain Isaac Relyea had lived at 54 Broad Street from 1895 to 1919.

Captain Isaac Relyea

Isaac Relyea was the owner and captain of the sailing sloop *Wade Hampton,* which was used to haul cargo among the Atlantic ports and occasionally traded in the West Indies. When not engaged in commerce, the sloop was used as a pleasure vessel, from which it was fashionable for ladies to watch the Carolina Yacht Club regatta in Charleston Harbor. In September 1897 Captain Relyea was returning with his boat from Wilmington during a storm when the sloop was broken to pieces on the north jetty near the harbor entrance. Relyea, his crew and two stowaways were rescued by the crew of the pilot boat *Cowan.* Previously, Relyea had been owner and master of the sloop *R.E. Lee.*

Isaac Relyea's father, Charles J. Relyea, was captain of the Confederate cargo boat *Planter* who, in violation of policy, was ashore with the other officers of the vessel the night enslaved wheelman Robert Smalls commandeered the ship and piloted his family and others past Fort Sumter to freedom. Smalls then turned over the *Planter* to the Union blockaders. Relyea was court martialed and found guilty of allowing the boat to be stolen. But the verdict was overturned by Confederate Maj. Gen. John C. Pemberton, commander of the Department of South Carolina, Georgia and Florida.

Since Charles J. Relyea lived on Tradd Street before being lost at sea in 1863, it is doubtful that he was the artist who painted on the walls of his son's property. Who did remains a mystery to this day.

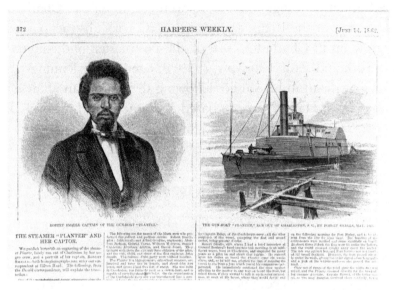

Robert Smalls, wheelman of the *CSS Planter*, which he piloted out of Charleston Harbor, May 1862. Courtesy Library of Congress.

The *Planter* was a rich prize. In addition to acquiring a valuable vessel and Small's expertise as a seasoned harbor pilot, the blockaders received marine charts and the boat's four rifled cannons, which were intended for harbor defense. Equally important, Federal authorities were told of the abandonment of strategically located Cole's Island, which protected the mouth of the Stono River and access to James Island. This intelligence precipitated a surprise Federal assault on James Island that ended with a Union defeat at Secessionville.

During Union Admiral Samuel Francis DuPont's ironclad attack in 1863 on Fort Sumter, Robert Smalls piloted the experimental tower ironclad USS *Keokuk*, which sustained heavy damage during the engagement and sank. Her two guns were salvaged by the Confederates under the noses of the blockading fleet. One of the *Keokuk*'s cannons is displayed in White Point Garden.

Artist Edward I.R. (Ned) Jennings also had his studio at 54½ Broad Street. Jennings was an important figure of the Charleston Renaissance of the 1920s, as one of the city's first abstract painters. He grew up in Charleston, son of the postmaster, and studied in New York and Paris. On May 7, 1929, aged thirty, Jennings shot himself to death in his studio, following the end of an affair with another man. Harlan Greene based a character, in his novel *Why We Never Danced the Charleston*, on Jennings.

Truth is...

According to misguided tradition, 54 Broad Street was built by master masons Peter and John Adam Horlbeck using materials left over from construction of the Exchange and Custom House, which was completed in 1771. A 1930 *News and Courier* article claimed 54 Broad was built with materials salvaged from a building that preceded the Exchange building. By 1936 another version said it was built with materials left over from the Exchange project. None of that is true.

New research indicates the building was built by John Paul Grimké, who bought the site in 1755, and in 1778 sold the lot with "the Brick Messuage or Tenement thereon Standing." The property later was owned by John Horlbeck Jr., son of John Adam Horlbeck, and was sold from his estate in 1846. That probably contributed to the Horlbeck legend.

The Italianate Trio

At 7, 9, and 11 Broad Street are three intriguing buildings in the mid-nineteenth century Italian Renaissance Revival style. The Connecticut brownstone façades of 9 and 11 Broad were executed by New York stonecutter W.G. Chave. Raised letters at No. 9 read "Exchange Office." In the curvilinear pediment at No. 11 are carvings of a globe, book, and scroll, indicating the building housed the S. G. Courtenay bookstore and publishing company.

The trio of Italianate Connecticut brownstone façades at 7, 9 and 11 Broad Street are often grouped together in photographs. This image shows 11 Broad Street converted into Robertson's Cafeteria. Courtesy Library of Congress.

7 Broad Street

Number 7 Broad Street was built in the 1850s for brokers William M. Martin and John C. Martin. The brownstone façade may mask an older structure. The Martins dealt primarily in real estate, insurance, and stock transactions. William Martin was also an attorney and alderman for Ward 3.

Before the war, John C. Martin was a captain in the Washington Artillery. Being thought too old for active duty, Martin joined the Charleston Regiment of Reserves and served in the defense of Charleston until mid-1864. He then served on active duty, guarding prisoners of war at Camp Sorghum in Columbia, protecting mountain passes in the Carolinas Campaign and participating in the Battle of Bentonville.

While at Camp Sorghum, he censored the inmates' outgoing mail and was well known to the captive Union officers. In October 1865, fearing that he might be arrested, Martin wrote one of his former prisoners, U.S. Col. Pennock Huey, asking for a job in Pennsylvania and to put in a good word for him if he were brought to trial. Then John Martin disappeared from history.

9 and 11 Broad Street

9 and 11 Broad Street were designed in 1856 by architect Edward Brickell White. The buildings have different versions of Codussian windows, named for Venetian Renaissance architect Mauro Codussi.

A West Point graduate, White was a surveyor, engineer, military man, and architect. Among his surviving public buildings in Charleston are Market Hall and the old South Carolina Electric and Gas building on Meeting Street. In 1850 he remodeled and expanded the College of Charleston main building, and designed the Porter's Lodge and the fence around the College Green. He designed the Huguenot Church, Grace Episcopal Church, Centenary Methodist Church, St. Johannes Lutheran Church, and St. Philip's steeple.

Number 9 Broad Street is a narrow, one-room-wide building designed for businessmen and brothers W. Pinkney Shingler and T.J. Shingler, from Orangeburg District.

W. Pinkney Shingler is not listed in Frances Leigh William's *The Founding Family; The Pinckneys of South Carolina*. This might explain the odd spelling of his middle name.

W. Pinkney Shingler built a mansion at 9 Limehouse Street on five lots that were once part of the Robert Limehouse tract. The interior has high ceilings, ornate plaster work, and handsome mantles. In front of the Italianate entrance, marble steps lead to a terrace enclosed by an iron railing designed by Christopher Werner, a German master craftsman whose works adorn many Charleston landmarks.

William Pinkney Shingler House, 9 Limehouse Street. Courtesy Library of Congress.

The Shingler brothers handled real estate transactions and speculated in cotton exports, a lucrative trade connected to Liverpool, Hamburg, and Marseilles. Information on cotton prices came to Charleston via telegraph. In 1857 cotton headquarters in Hamburg sent a confusing report that alarmed W. Pinkney Shingler. Thinking he had suffered a serious financial reversal, Shingler sold his house to his brother-in-law, James Addison, for $23,000, a high price at the time. When he discovered that the information was incorrect, Shingler bought three lots on the east side of Limehouse Street and built an even larger mansion in 1858.

W. Pinkney Shingler married three times: first to Harriet English, then to her sister Caroline, and finally to Susan Ball Venning. A charming family tradition is that Caroline English refused to live in her deceased sister's house, which is why Shingler sold Number 9 Limehouse Street and built Number 10 across the street for Caroline. It might even be true.

In addition to being a factor, W. Pinkney Shingler was a planter in Christ Church Parish. He represented the parish at the 1860 Secession Convention, where he signed the Ordinance of Secession.

Shingler served under Brig. Gen. Barnard Elliott Bee, Jr. at First Manassas (Union forces called it the Battle of Bull Run), which the Confederates won. Bee was the first Confederate general to be killed in the war. It was he who referred to Gen. Thomas J. Jackson and his men as a "stone wall" during the battle.

After First Manassas, Shingler returned to South Carolina and formed an infantry/cavalry unit that saw action on Edisto Island in March 1862. He was later promoted to colonel in command of the 7th South Carolina Cavalry and fought at Drury's Bluff and in the Petersburg campaign. At the end of the war, he returned to South Carolina and commanded the state militia. Shingler took the U.S. loyalty oath in 1865 and became a state senator (1865-1867). He died in 1869 and was buried in the Venning family cemetery in Mount Pleasant.

Miss Sue Frost's Office

9 Broad Street continued to make history in the 20th century when it became the real estate office of Susan ("Miss Sue") Pringle Frost, the second woman in the state to have a real estate license and the first woman in Charleston's history to own a real estate office. Daughter of Dr. Francis LeJau Frost and Rebecca Brewton Pringle, she was descended from Santee River rice planters. She was born in the Miles Brewton House on lower King Street and grew up there.

Susan Pringle Frost. Courtesy Preservation Society of Charleston.

When her father's phosphate fertilizer business failed and the region's rice cultivation declined, she learned stenography and worked for architect Bradford Lee Gilbert, designer of the 1901 South Carolina Inter-State and West Indian Exposition. She was active in the women's suffrage movement that promoted the 19th Amendment, giving women the right to vote, and lobbied for the admission of women to the College of Charleston. Her passion, however, was saving Charleston's historic homes from demolition or defacement.

After learning that Standard Oil planned to raze Joseph Manigault's mansion on Meeting Street, Miss Sue gathered thirty-two ladies and several gentlemen to 20 South Battery, home of her cousin Nell McColl Pringle. On the afternoon of April 21, 1920, the Society for the Preservation of Old Dwellings (now the Preservation Society) was born. Miss Sue also collaborated with Mayor Thomas

Miles Brewton House, 27 King Street, Courtesy Library of Congress.

P. Stoney and architect Albert Simons in establishing the Old and Historic District and the Board of Architectural Review in 1931.

In 1985 realtors Lois Lane and Ruthie Smythe restored 9 Broad Street to its original architectural design, with doorways and arches in cast brownstone. Signage about Miss Sue Frost's occupancy is posted inside near the entrance. A Preservation Society historical marker was placed on the building in 2020.

11 Broad Street

Number 11 Broad Street was designed for bookseller Samuel Courtenay. Tradition says that William Gilmore Simms — Charleston's famed poet, novelist, historian, and editor — wrote portions of his novels in the bookstore. It is said he would request a pencil and paper, stand at a counter, and write the latest installment of his work, which subsequently was published serially in the *Southern Literary Gazette*. In 1912, E.H. Robertson Cigar Company occupied 11 Broad Street, and in 1941, the first floor and façade were remodeled as Robertson's Cafeteria, which became a meeting place for Charleston's political and business leaders.

A Garden that Grew into a Bank

In 1955 South Carolina National Bank (SCNB), which was at the northeast corner of State and Broad streets at the time, commissioned the late Samuel Gaillard Stoney to write a book about its history. No one could foresee events that later enabled the bank to expand its operations all the way to East Bay Street.

Painting of the Exchange, by Alicia Rhett, ca. 1970, shows the bank garden in the foreground. Courtesy Aubrey Hancock. Photograph by Richard P. Donohoe.

On New Year's Eve 1963, a spectacular, wind-whipped blaze destroyed the Marcus Building, a three-story commercial building at the northwest corner of Broad and East Bay streets, containing the Marcus Rexall Drug Store. Within weeks, a wooden barricade around the site was erected and the building's owner, John B. Marcus, announced plans to construct an eight-to-ten story replacement. Because of difficulty in obtaining financing, the barricade remained in situ for more than a year before it raised the ire of City Council and was replaced with a wire fence, also an eyesore. The following month the site was up for sale.

The Park

The vacant corner site was purchased by SCNB, which planned to build an eleven-story wing adjacent to its Broad Street offices. Although zoning permitted increased height, the size and scale were criticized by preservationists. The bank created a garden on the site after plans for the high-rise failed to materialize.

The beautiful garden and park was across the street from the Old Exchange. A fountain in the center of a circular pool was surrounded by a pathway using approximately 20,000 old Charleston bricks from the South Carolina National Bank branch at 558 King Street. In January 1975, the park was opened to the public.

Buildings left intact after the Marcus fire. Courtesy Library of Congress.

The bank finally received city approval and in 1982 completed a new addition on the garden site. In preparation for the 19,000-square-foot addition, the garden had been cleared and the shrubbery donated to St. Stephen's Church. The new addition was designed by architect James H. Small III. It completed the occupation of the block of Broad Street that the bank had begun in 1817.

The bank began as the Office of Discount and Deposit, which was South Carolina's branch of the Second Bank of the United States. The institution was established in 1817 and constructed the bank building at 16 Broad Street, at the corner of State Street, with the iconic American eagle in its pediment. When President Andrew Jackson forced closure of the Second Bank in 1834, a group of Charleston men received a state charter for the Bank of Charleston, which acquired the building and employed the same banking staff as its predecessor. The Bank of Charleston merged with smaller banks in Columbia and Greenville in 1926 to form the South Carolina National Bank (SCNB). Over time the bank expanded its facilities northward along State Street and eastward along Broad Street. Wachovia acquired SCNB in 1991 and Wachovia, in turn, was acquired by Wells Fargo Bank in 2004.

Streetscape when there were a series of commercial buildings located on the north side of Broad Street between East Bay and State Streets. From *Art Work of Charleston*, part 9. Published 1893.

Eagle in pediment, Second Bank of the United States, 16 Broad Street. Courtesy Library of Congress

Ripley's Believe It or Not

Robert Ripley, an American cartoonist and entrepreneur, had a syndicated newspaper cartoon called "Ripley's Believe It or Not" that, beginning in 1929, was published in newspapers nationwide. His panel dated June 5, 1939, featured "The Corner of Four Laws" at Charleston's Broad and Meeting streets. On that date, the panel was published in *The News and Courier* and other papers. A story in the same edition of the newspaper stated that, "The drawing of the church was based on a photograph sent to Ripley." According to a letter in the Ripley archives, information about the famous intersection was in a letter sent in by Jimmy O. Lane, a taxi driver and tour guide.

The name stuck, and today it is known as the Four Corners of Law. The intersection a is focal point with City Hall representing local law, the Charleston County Court House representing state law, the U.S. Post Office and Court House representing national law, and St. Michael's Church representing divine law.

This cartoon was based on a photograph sent by *The News and Courier,* with information provided by Jimmy O. Lane, a Charleston tour guide. Courtesy Ripley Entertainment Inc.

The Hat Man

The Plenge Building is at the southeast corner of Broad and Church streets. Charles Plenge, who bought the property in 1870, was the consummate promoter of his clothing store. He modified his new acquisition by adding an Italianate façade topped with a pressed-tin cornice that proclaimed Plenge ownership.

The Hat Man. Courtesy The Charleston Museum.

To promote his haberdashery, there was a painting of a clown-like man sporting a top hat on the Church Street wall. "Plenge the Hatman" also appeared on trading cards that promoted the latest fall styles from Fifth Avenue including "Fine Silk hats, $4.00, $5.00 — Men's Soft Hats, 50 cts to $5.00 — Men's Stiff Hats $1.00 to $3.50 — NOBBY HATS FOR YOUNG MEN, a specialty" and "Silk, Alpaca and Gingham UMBRELLA prices, Mourning Bands Put on Hats, 25 Cents."

But the image of the hat man was painted over and forgotten. Fortunately, when the building's wall was sandblasted in the 1930s, the artwork was rediscovered and restored. The image catches the eye because his face and body are comprised of a wide variety of old-fashioned hats. Charlestonians call him "The Hat Man."

The Public Common

In 1768, Gov. Charles Greville, Lord Montagu, and the Commons House of Assembly created a public area primarily to provide a safe and convenient place to anchor vessels on the west side of town during storms. Commissioners were appointed to oversee cutting a six-foot-wide channel in the tidal marsh from the west end of Broad Street to the low-water mark of the Ashley River.

The Revolution intervened, and when Charleston was incorporated in 1783, the public common fell under the jurisdiction of the city council. Little was done until 1817 when the city sold a tract between present-day Broad and Tradd Streets to Joshua Brown, who built a sawmill on the Ashley River, then sold his interests to Alexander Hext Chisolm around 1829. Chisolm developed a thriving rice and lumber mill complex on the river and built a handsome Greek Revival mansion nearby at 172 Tradd Street. By January 1861, according to an article in *The New York Times*, Chisolm's rice mill was the largest in the United States.

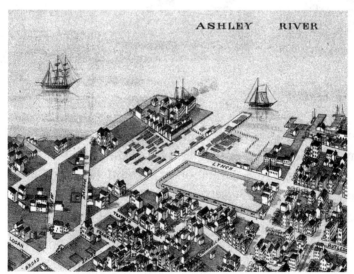

Detail from C.N. Drie's 1872 "Bird's Eye View" of Charleston. Courtesy Library of Congress.

The west wing of a Chisolm mill building, ca. 1859, survives as part of the United States Coast Guard complex at the west end of Tradd Street. Also surviving is the ca. 1840 Chisolm Mills superintendent's house at 190 Tradd Street.

Meanwhile, the city extended Broad Street westward and continued to subdivide and lease tracts on the Colonial Common primarily to lumber interests. The 1872 "Bird's Eye View of Charleston" illustrates the Broad Street extension, the Rutledge Street Pond (renamed Colonial Lake in 1881), Chisolm's house, rice mill, and holding ponds for timber.

Colonial Lake beside Broad Street. Courtesy Library of Congress.

In 1909 the city began to fill the Ashley River mud flats on the southwest side of the peninsula. Called the "Boulevard Project," this endeavor created a retaining wall and roadway along present-day Murray Boulevard extending from White Point Garden and curving northwestward to the west end of Tradd Street.

A 1902 Sanborn insurance map of Charleston, updated through 1929, shows half the block bounded by Broad, Ashley, Tradd, and Chisolm streets being used for storage by Anderson Lumber Company and half occupied by private residences. According to local tradition, the primary fill for the marshland was wood chips and sawdust from the lumber mill.

Anderson Lumber Company

In 1875 Patrick P. Toale leased a tract near what is now Moultrie Playground adjacent to the Broad Street Pond for another lumber mill. This triggered a lawsuit challenging the city's continuing practice of shrinking the public common. The suit was resolved by an 1881 ordinance that decreed the remaining public common marshlands dedicated in 1768 be kept for the people of Charleston, but Toale's lease was allowed to continue. Toale's mill was a thriving concern when his unexpired lease was transferred to Anderson Lumber Company.

The Andersons arrived in Charleston with impressive credentials, and it was not long before their lumber company played a prominent role in changing the landscape on the east end of Broad street during the turn-of-the-century.

An ancestor, Gen. Robert Anderson, figured prominently in the development of the Pendleton area of South Carolina, and Anderson County is named in his honor. He served in the American Revolution and as a judge, state representative, and lieutenant governor.

Robert Anderson's second wife was Lydia Turpin Maverick, widow of Samuel Maverick, a prominent Charleston merchant. Elizabeth Anderson, a daughter from Robert Anderson's first marriage, wedded Lydia Maverick's son Samuel Maverick Jr. Their son, Samuel Augustus (Gus) Maverick, later migrated to Texas and became one of the largest land and cattle owners in the world. He was a signer of the Texas Declaration of Independence and his portrait hangs in the Texas Hall of Fame.

It is said that Gus Maverick's lackadaisical overseer failed to brand his cattle, and cowboys soon learned that when they saw an unbranded steer, it belonged to the Maverick herd. Thus the word "maverick" — which means "an unorthodox or independent-minded person" — continues in our language today. Charleston's Maverick family was descended from John Maverick, who arrived from Barbados in the 1670s and was appointed by the Lords Proprietors to the Grand Council.

One of General Anderson's great grandsons, dentist Dr. John Anderson moved to Charleston in the 1840s. His oldest son, Robert Maxwell Anderson, was the entrepreneur heavily involved in the lumber industry, serving as president of Anderson Lumber Company and president of Anderson Spool and Bobbin Manufacturing Company. He developed Colonial Street and built a row of houses on the south side of Calhoun Street and tenement housing on Maverick Street. He was also president of the United States Industrial Life Insurance Company and vice president of the State Savings Bank.

Anderson Lumber Company was forced to close its mill when the Toale lease expired in 1929. The remains of the boiler house that once powered the mill can be found in a thicket at the foot of Barre Street. The holding pond north of Broad Street was filled in and dedicated as Moultrie Playground in 1930. The former company office at 305 Broad Street has walls faced with milled wood that showcase the extensive capabilities of the firm.

Fritz's Gracious Gesture

The U.S. Post Office and Courthouse, a Renaissance Revival building, was funded by Congress in 1887. It replaced the Guard House, which was wrecked by the 1886 Earthquake. Construction began in 1889 and was completed in 1896.

An inaccurate plaque on the Broad Street front of the building states that it was designed by Charleston architect John Henry Devereux. The building actually was designed by federal staff architects under the direction of the Superintending Architect of the Treasury. Will Freret, a New Orleans architect, was in that post when the building was designed. Devereux might have been the local supervising architect.

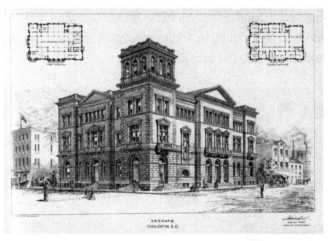

U. S. Post Office and Courthouse. Drawings from the Office of the Superintending Architect of the U.S. Treasury. Courtesy Library of Congress.

The building is constructed of Winnsboro blue granite, one of the finest building materials in the world. The public rooms are splendidly finished with red Brazilian marble, Santo Domingan mahogany, and brown marble stairs with elaborate brass railings.

An elevator in a brass cage was added later. A quaint Post Office Museum is located on the main level.

The J. Waties Waring Judicial Center

Attached to the Post Office, next to the park, at 83 Meeting Street, is the J. Waties Waring Judicial Center, designed by architect Garey Goff and completed in 1987. The center originally was named for U.S. Senator Ernest F. (Fritz) Hollings who, in a generous gesture, asked in 2015 that it be renamed for Judge Waring. Judge Waring was honored, after decades of being scorned by Charleston traditionalists for his key rulings advancing civil rights. His dissenting opinion in a 1951 case with the phrase, "Segregation is per se inequality," became the basis for the U.S. Supreme Court ruling in ground-breaking U.S. Supreme Court decision called *Brown vs. The Board of Education of Topeka* in 1954. The legal community erected a marker on Meeting Street outlining Judge Waring's contributions to civil rights. In addition, a statue of the judge was placed in the park adjacent to the building.

South side of the U.S. Post Office with the Post Office Park where the Waring Judicial Building now sits. Courtesy Library of Congress.

Burbage's

Burbage's corner store is a Charleston institution that was first opened in 1946 by Robert Ackerman Burbage and his brother John Henry on Ashley Avenue. Burbage was a farmer's son from New Hope, near Summerville, before serving overseas in World War II. When he returned, his brother met him at the train station saying, "Don't unpack, we're going to Charleston." They did just that and were in business together until his brother decided to go into business elsewhere.

Robert Burbage opted to open his own grocery on Tradd Street, then relocated to two other places on the street. The grocery was a huge success partly because of the goodwill he created with his customers young and old.

Burbage's, the last corner grocery store on Broad Street (still open for business). Photograph by Richard P. Donohoe.

Eve Meddin Berlinsky's father, who delivered meat to the grocery, remembers "Mr. Burbage" fondly, saying he was the ultimate Southern gentleman. "He never forgot your name, whether you were there every day or every year. He even delivered ice cream to the 'rotten' kids who ordered without their parents' knowledge."

In 1961 Burbage moved the store to 157 Broad Street. When he learned that he had throat cancer, he sold the store to his son, Al, who expanded the store's offerings with a variety of made-to-order deli sandwiches and soups and spreads like "Big Al's Pimiento Cheese." Al and his wife Myrtis moved into the apartment over the grocery store. Myrtis Burbage ran a barber shop a few blocks east on Broad Street next to Berlin's Clothiers.

By the time Al Burbage decided to retire, his self-serve store and meat market had been in the family for more than sixty-seven years. Sadly, without any successors to inherit the business, it was sold to new owners.

Enter George and Lisa Bowen of West Ashley. They had been looking for a commercial project for more than a year. The timing was perfect. George Bowen had once owned two corner stores on the peninsula: Queen Street Grocery and George's Grocery at Beaufain and Coming streets. He had sold the stores in the early 1990s and gone to work for the Piggly Wiggly supermarket chain.

Capitalizing on a vintage model grocery has obviously worked. Customers come from all walks of life, and the Burbage tradition continues to thrive.

William Moultrie

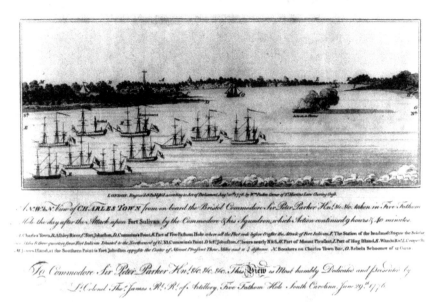

"A view of Charles Town from on board the *Bristol* ... taken in Five Fathom Hole the day after the attack upon Fort Sullivan by the Commodore & his squadron, which action continued 9 hours & 40 minutes." Courtesy Library of Congress.

The General William Moultrie Playground, at the west end of Broad Street, is named for William Moultrie, whose importance in South Carolina history cannot be over-emphasized.

Born in Charles Town, Moultrie was the second son of a prominent Scottish physician immigrant who became a member of the elite planter society. One of many old Charleston names, the family name Moultrie properly is pronounced "Mool-trie" not "Mol-trie" as is frequently heard.

At age nineteen, William married Damaris Elizabeth de St. Ju lien, who inherited Northampton plantation, in St. John's, Berkeley, Parish. Under the law of the day, the plantation became the husband's property. Thus for a ring and a kiss, he owned a rice plantation and two hundred slaves. He eventually acquired thousands of acres throughout South Carolina and North Carolina.

Young Moultrie was drawn to public service and at age twenty-one was elected to the Commons House of Assembly for St. John's, Berkeley, Parish. It was the start of a lifelong political career. He was later elected to the Continental Congress and served in the state House of Representatives and Senate and as lieutenant governor once and governor twice. His last post was as treasurer for Lower South Carolina, from which he resigned in 1804 because of ill health.

A citizen-soldier, he participated in the Cherokee Wars, including service as Gov. William Henry Lyttleton's aide-de-camp in 1759. By 1774, Moultrie held the rank of colonel of the militia. When the American Revolution broke out, the Provincial Congress selected him as commander of the Second South Carolina Regiment of Foot.

General William Moultrie (1730–1805), by Rembrandt Peale. Courtesy Gibbes Museum of Art/Carolina Art Association.

By March of 1776, Colonel Moultrie was the commanding officer of militia forces ordered to secure Sullivan's Island and complete the construction of a fort built in preparation for an expected British naval attack. It was feared that if the British captured Sullivan's Island, they could use it as a staging area for an assault on the city.

Continental Army Maj. Gen. Charles Henry Lee of Virginia, commanding general of Patriot forces defending Charles Town, arrived for inspection. Thinking the British cannon would cut the crude palmetto log fort apart, he asked Moultrie how the men would shelter themselves from the British fire? Moultrie replied calmly, "We will lie behind the ruins and prevent their men from landing." Incensed, Lee departed and asked Gov. John Rutledge to order the fort dismantled. Fortunately, Rutledge declined, and the rest is history.

On the morning of June 28, 1776, a British fleet of nine warships with 300 cannons, stood off the southern tip of Sullivan's Island, bombarding the fort. However, the British cannonballs had little destructive effect on Fort Sullivan's walls of palmetto logs and sand. The Patriot artillery had only thirty-one cannons but the defenders expertly directed their fire to cause great damage to the British fleet.

THE ATTACK ON SULLIVAN'S ISLAND

British fleet's attack on Fort Sullivan. Courtesy New York Public Library.

Admiral Sir Peter Parker, the British fleet commander, was humiliated by having his breeches torn off by a flying splinter. William, Lord Campbell, the last Royal governor, was wounded by a splinter in his side. He never recovered and died two years later in London. The HMS *Acteon* was grounded and abandoned, and several other ships badly damaged.

A smaller Patriot force, under Col. William Thompson, defended the north end of Sullivan's Island. They prevented British troops that had landed on Long Island (now Isle of Palms) from crossing Breech Inlet. Thompson's task was made easier by a British miscalculation about the depth of the inlet; they expected several inches of water and encountered several feet.

The Battle of Fort Sullivan also witnessed the valor of Sgt. William Jasper. When the Patriot flag was shot down, Jasper risked his life by jumping onto the rampart to restore it.

Sargent Jasper Monument in White Point Garden. Courtesy New York Public Library.

At sunset, the British fleet retreated and limped back to New York. The British would not return to South Carolina until 1779. It is said that news of the Fort Sullivan victory reached Philadelphia in time to influence the Continental Congress in signing the Declaration of Independence.

Moultrie was hailed as an American hero, and the Continental Congress voted to promote him to brigadier general. Moultrie saw action throughout South Carolina, but most of his attention was devoted to defending Charles Town. When Charles Town fell in May 1780, Moultrie was among the 5,000 Patriots captured.

Charles Greville, Lord Montagu, second son of Robert Montagu, Duke of Manchester, was Royal governor of South Carolina, 1766-1769. Moultrie befriended the young governor, who was popular in Charles Town; Montagu Street was named for him in 1770. Afterwards, Montagu was appointed to recruit American prisoners of war to form a corps to capture Nicaragua from the Spanish, who were allies of the American Patriots. Promised that they would not have to fight other Americans, many accepted the tempting offer. Then he approached General Moultrie.

In a famous exchange of letters, Lord Montagu argued that General Moultrie could honorably quit the revolution and move to Jamaica to sit out the war. Moultrie rejected the offer, with indignation:

"Would you wish to have that man, whom you have honored with your friendship, play the traitor? Surely not! You say, by quitting this country, for a short time, I might avoid disagreeable conversations, and might return at my own leisure, and take possession of my estates for myself and family; but, you have forgotten to tell me, how am I to get rid of the feelings of an injured, honest heart, and where to hide myself from myself!...The repossessing of my estates; the offer of the command of your Regiment, and the honor you propose of serving under me, are paltry considerations to the loss of my reputation! No! not the fee simple of that valuable Island of Jamaica should induce me to part with my integrity!"

Moultrie remained a prisoner of war, exiled to British-occupied Philadelphia, until he was exchanged for Maj. Gen. John Burgoyne in 1782. Burgoyne, who was perhaps a better playwright than a general, had been captured in 1777 at Saratoga by Gen. Horatio Gates, who later commanded Continental forces in South Carolina. The British defeat at Saratoga convinced the French to enter the war on the side of the Americans.

In 1802, Moultrie published *Memoirs of the American Revolution*, still considered the best firsthand account of the struggle for independence. He died in Charleston on September 27, 1805. He was buried in the family cemetery on his son's property at Windsor Hill north of Charleston.

Moultrie's legacy has been honored in many ways in the Charleston area. Fort Sullivan was renamed Fort Moultrie, and on June 28, 1978, his remains were re-interred at the Fort Moultrie Visitor Center. A life-size statue of Moultrie in White Point Garden, sculpted by Charleston artist John Michel, faces the fort he bravely defended. The palmetto was added to the South Carolina flag in honor of its effectiveness against British cannon fire. And every year since 1777, on June 28, Charlestonians have celebrated Carolina Day. Representatives of the city's civic organizations meet in Washington Square, just off Broad Street. They form a parade ranked by the age of the organizations and march down Meeting Street to White Point Garden, where the crowd, usually wilting from the heat, stands and listens to speeches.

Contributed by L. Mendel Rivers, Jr.

Moultrie Playground

In 1922, the City of Charleston began a landfill program on the west side of the peninsula, including the marsh lands between Colonial Lake and the Ashley River. Envisioned as a possible playground, a park opened in 1930. The playground, quite naturally, was named after the great Revolutionary War hero, William Moultrie.

Fast forward to 2007 when Darla Moore, one of the state's most accomplished businesswomen, founded and was the initial benefactor of the Charleston Parks Conservancy. In 2008-2009, the Conservancy began plans for redevelopment of Colonial Lake and the adjacent Moultrie Playground.

Twentieth Century naval warfare was vastly different from that of Moultrie's time. The U.S.S. *L. Mendel Rivers* nuclear attack submarine (since decommissioned) heads down river towards the old Cooper River bridges as it leaves for the open seas. Courtesy Captain Bradford N. McDonald, 1994.

When the City and the Charleston Parks Conservancy agreed that capital donors could be recognized with a plaque, Steve and Ann Rhodes decided to honor a "man of color" who had made significant contributions to horticulture, George Washington Carver, whose accomplishments are enumerated on the plaque.

Bibliography

Aiken, David. *Fire in the Cradle; Charleston's Literary Heritage*. Charleston: Charleston Press, 1999.

Alleyne, Warren & Henry Fraser. *The Barbados-Carolina Connection*. Singapore: Wordsmith International Inc., second edition, 2016.

Annan, Jason and Pamela Gabriel. *The Great Cooper River Bridge*. Columbia: University of South Carolina Press, 2002.

Bailey, N. Louise and Elizabeth Ivey Cooper. *Biographical Directory of the South Carolina House of Representatives, Volume III: 1775-1790*. Columbia: University of South Carolina Press, 1981.

Bailey, N. Louise. *Biographical Directory of the South Carolina House of Representatives, Volume IV: 1791-1815*. Columbia: University of South Carolina Press, 1984.

Ball, William Watts. *The State That Forgot: South Carolina's Surrender to Democracy*. Indianapolis: Bobbs-Merrill Company, 1932.

Bell, Malcolm, Jr. *Major Butler's Legacy, Five Generations of a Slaveholding Family*. Athens: University of Georgia Press, 1987.

Boggs, Doyle W. *The Amazing Mayor Grace; John P. Grace and the Making of Modern Charleston, 1874-1940*. Charleston: Evening Post Books, 2012.

Bowden, David K. *The Execution of Isaac Hayne*. Lexington, SC: Sandlapper Publishing, 1977.

Brandon, Edgar Ewing, ed. *A Pilgrimage of Liberty; A Contemporary Account of the Triumphal Tour of General Lafayette Through the Southern and Western States in 1825, as Reported by the Local Newspapers*. Athens, OH: The Lawhead Press, 1944.

Butler, Nicholas Michael. *Votaries of Apollo, The St. Cecilia Society and the Patronage of Concert Music in Charleston, South Carolina 1765-1820*. Columbia: University of South Carolina Press, 2007.

Cochran, Valentina. "Separate But Equal?: A Lesson on the *Briggs v. Elliott* Case in Clarendon County, South Carolina." www.teachingushistory.org/lessons/separatebutequal.html

Coulton, E. Merton. *George Walton Williams: The Life of a Southern Merchant and Banker, 1820-1907*. Athens,: Hibriten Press, 1976.

Dalcho, Frederick. *An Historical Account of the Protestant Episcopal Church in South Carolina from the first settlement of the province to the War of the Revolution*. Charleston: E. Thayer, 1820.

Defenbaugh, Kayleigh Anne. "Living and Working on the Peninsula: A Study of Spatial Home and Work Location Relationships as Related to Occupations and Charleston's Historic Landscape at the Turn of the Twentieth Century." Thesis Presented to the Graduate Schools of Clemson University and the College of Charleston In Partial Fulfillment of the Requirements for the Degree Master of Science Historic Preservation, 2020.

Easterby, J. H. *A History of the College of Charleston Founded 1770*. New York: The Scribner Press, 1935.

Easterby, J. H. *History of the St. Andrew's Society of Charleston, South Carolina 1729-1929*. Charleston: Walker, Evans & Cogswell Company, 1929.

Eastman, Margaret Middleton Rivers. *Hidden History of Civil War Charleston*. Charleston: History Press, 2012.

Eastman, Margaret Middleton Rivers, Richard Donohoe & Maurice Eugenie Horne Thompson, with Robert P. Stockton. *The Huguenot Church in Charleston*. Charleston: History Press, 2018.

Edgar, Walter B. *South Carolina: A History*. Columbia: University of South Carolina Press, 1998.

Edgar, Walter B., ed. *The South Carolina Encyclopedia*. Columbia: University of South Carolina Press, 2006.

Edgar, Walter B., N. Louise Bailey, and Inez Watson. *Biographical Directory of the South Carolina House of Representatives, Volume II: The Commons House of Assembly, 1692-1775*. Columbia: University of South Carolina Press, 1977.

Fant, Jennie Holton. *The Travelers' Charleston; Accounts of Charleston and Lowcountry, South Carolina, 1666-1861*. Columbia: University of South Carolina Press, 2016.

Ford, Frederick A. *Census of the City of Charleston, South Carolina, For the Year 1861*. Illustrated by Statistical Tables. Prepared under the Authority of the City Council. Charleston: Steam-Power Presses of Evans & Cogswell, 1861.

Freehling, William. *The Road to Disunion, Volume II: Secessionists Triumphant 1854-1861*. New York: Oxford University Press, 2007.

Giles, Katherine W. "A Hurricane of Fire; The Great Charleston Fire of 1861," *Carologue, A Publication of the South Carolina Historical Society*, 27, no. 3 (Winter 2011) 22.

Greene, Harlan M. *Mr. Skylark: John Bennett and the Charleston Renaissance*. Athens: University of Georgia Press, 2001.

Hart, Emma. *Building Charleston; Town and Society in the Eighteenth-Century British Atlantic World*. Charlottesville: University of Virginia Press, 2010.

Historical Sketch of the Confederate Home and College. Charleston: Walker, Evans & Cogswell, 1921.

Hicks, Brian. *The Mayor: Joe Riley and the Rise of Charleston*. Charleston: Evening Post Books, 2015.

Hine, William C. "The 1867 Charleston Streetcar Sit-ins; A Case of Successful Black Protest." *South Carolina Historical Magazine 77* (April 1976): 110-114.

History of South Carolina. Yates Snowden and Harry Gardner Cutler, Eds. 5 vols. Chicago and New York: The Lewis Publishing Co., 1920.

Hutchisson, James M., and Harlan Green, eds. *Renaissance in Charleston*. Athens: University of Georgia Press, 2003.

Joyner, Charles. *Down by the Riverside; A South Carolina Slave Community*. Urbana: University of Illinois Press, 1984.

Klinck, Isabella S. *Personal Experiences of the Great Charleston Earthquake*. North Liberty, Iowa: Ice Cube Press, 2003.

Lipscomb, Terry. *George Washington's Southern Tour*. Columbia: South Carolina Department of Archives and History, 2011.

Lounsbury, Carl R. *From Statehouse to Courthouse; An Architectural History of South Carolina's Colonial Capitol and Charleston County Courthouse*. Columbia: University of South Carolina Press, 2001.

Mazyck, Arthur, and Gene Waddell. *Charleston in 1883*. Easley, SC: Southern Historical Press, 1983.

McCrady, Edward. *The History of South Carolina Under the Proprietary Government, 1670-1719*. New York: The Macmillan Company, 1897.

McCrady, Edward. *The History of South Carolina Under the Royal Government, 1719-1776*. New York: The Macmillan Company, 1899.

McCrady, Edward. *The History of South Carolina in the Revolution 1775–1780*. New York: Macmillan Company, 1901.

McCrady, Edward. *The History of South Carolina in the Revolution 1780-1783*. New York: The Macmillan Company, 1902.

[McElveen, A. J.]. *Broke by the War; Letters of a Slave Trader*. Ed. Edmund L. Drago. Columbia: University of South Carolina Press, 1993.

McLaughlin, J. Michael, and Lee Davis Todman. *It Happened in South Carolina*. Gilford, CT: Globe Pequot Press, 2003.

Middleton, Margaret Simons. *David and Martha Laurens Ramsey*. New York: Carlton Press, Inc., 1971.

Millar, Sarah, and Stephen G. Hoffius. *Upheaval in Charleston: Earthquake and Murder on the Eve of Jim Crow*. Athens: University of Georgia Press, 2011.

Miller, Ruth M., and Ann Taylor Andrus. *Charleston's Old Exchange Building, A Witness to American History*. Charleston: History Press, 2005.

Morgan, James Morris. *Recollections of a Rebel Reefer*. New York: Houghton Mifflin Company, 1917.

Nepveux, Ethel Trenholm Seabrook. *George Alfred Trenholm and the Company that Went to War*. Anderson, SC: Electric City Printing Company, 1994.

Pease, William H. and Jane H. Pease. *James Louis Petigru, Southern Conservative, Southern Dissident*. Athens: University of Georgia Press, 1995; Columbia: University of South Carolina Press, 2002.

Pease, Jane H. and William H. Pease. *A Family of Women; The Carolina Petigrus in Peace and War*. Chapel Hill: University of North Carolina Press, 1999.

"Porgy and Bess Bring Back Memories of Sammy Smalls." *The News and Courier*, October 14, 1985.

Porter, A. Toomer. *Led On! Step by Step*. 100th Anniversary Edition. New York: Arno Press, 1967.

Ravenel, Beatrice St. Julien. *Architects of Charleston*. Charleston: Carolina Art Association, 1945, rev. 1964. Columbia: University of South Carolina Press, 1992.

Ravenel, Mrs. St. Julien. *Charleston: The Place and the People*. New York: Macmillan, 1906.

Rivers, Margaret Middleton, Margaret Middleton Rivers Eastman, and L. Mendel Rivers, Jr. *Mendel and Me: Life with Congressman L. Mendel Rivers*. Charleston: History Press, 2007.

Robinson, Roxana. "The Strange Career of Frank Dawson," *New York Times*, March 20, 2012.

Rogers, David. *Charleston; The Antebellum Neighborhoods and Buildings*. Summerville, SC: The Joggling Board Press, 2020.

Rogers, George C., Jr. *Charleston in the Age of the Pinckneys*. Norman: University of Oklahoma Press, 1969; Columbia: University of South Carolina Press, 1980.

Rosen, Robert N. *A Short History of Charleston, South Carolina*. San Francisco: Lexicos, 1982; Charleston: Peninsula Press, 1992; Columbia: University of South Carolina Press, 1997.

Rowe, Charles R. *Pages of History: 200 Years of the Post and Courier*. Charleston: Evening Post Publishing Company, 2003.

Sass, Herbert Ravenel. *Outspoken: 160 Years of The News and Courier*. Columbia: University of South Carolina Press, 1958.

Simons, Albert and Samuel Lapham, Jr. *The Early Architecture of Charleston*. New York: Press of the American Institute of Architects, 1927; Columbia: University of South Carolina Press, 1970.

Simons, Harriet P. and Albert Simons. "The William Burrows House of Charleston." *Winterthur Portfolio*, 3 (1967) 172-203.

Smith, Alice R. Huger and Daniel E. Huger Smith. *The Dwelling Houses of Charleston, South Carolina*. Philadelphia: J.B. Lippencott Company, 1917; Charleston: History Press, 2007.

Smith, Henry A.M. *The Historical Writings of Henry A.M. Smith*. 3 vols. Spartanburg, SC: The Reprint Company, Publishers, in association with the South Carolina Historical Society, 1988.

Sodders, Richard Phillip. "The Theatre Management of Alexandre Placide in Charleston, 1794-1812." LSU Historical Digital Commons, 1983, 127-128.

Steedman, Margurite. "Charleston's Forgotten Tea Party." *The Georgia Review* (Volume XXI, Number 27, Summer 1967).

Stockton, Robert P. *The Great Shock; The Effects of the 1886 Earthquake on the Built Environment of Charleston, South Carolina*. Easley, SC: Southern Historical Press, 1986.

Stokes, Karen. *The Immortal 600; Surviving Civil War Charleston and Savannah*. Charleston: History Press, 2013.

Stono; Documenting and Interpreting a Southern Slave Revolt. Ed. Mark M. Smith. Columbia: University of South Carolina Press, 2005.

Thomson, Jack. *Charleston at War; The Photographic Record, 1860-1865*. Gettysburg: Thomas Publications, 2000.

Tobias, Thomas J. *The Hebrew Orphan Society of Charleston, S.C. founded 1801*. Charleston: Published by the Society, 1957.

Waddell, Gene. *Charleston Architecture, 1670-1860*. Charleston: Wyrick & Company, 2003.

Walsh, Richard. Sons *of Liberty, A Study of the Artisans 1763-1789*. Columbia: University of South Carolina Press, 1959.

Williams, Alfred B. *Hampton and His Red Shirts — South Carolina's Deliverance in 1876*. Charleston: Walker, Evans & Cogswell, 1935.

Williams, George W. *Early Ministers at St. Michael's, Charleston*. Charleston: The Dalcho Historical Society, 1961.

Williams, George W. *St. Michael's 1751-1951; With Supplements 1951-2001*. Charleston: College of Charleston Library, 2001.

Willis, Eola. *The Charleston Stage in the XVIII Century: With Social Settings of the Time*. Columbia, SC: The State, 1924.

Year Book 1881, City of Charleston. Charleston: Walker, Evans & Cogswell Company for the City Council of Charleston, 1881.

William and Mary, 21
Williams, George Walton,
166, *257*, 257-259
Williamson, Andrew, 66-67
Willoughby, William (Lord
Willoughby), 5
Wilson, Woodrow, 222
Wilton, Joseph, 60
Work House, 17-18, *18*
Wrighten, Charlotte
Sophia, 77-78

Y
Yeamans, John, *5*, 5-6, 8,
45
Yeamans, Margaret
Berringer, *5*, 5-6
Yemassee War, 27
Young, Elizabeth Jenkins
(Liz), 42-43

About the Authors

Margaret (Peg) Middleton Rivers Eastman

A Charlestonian by birth, Peg is actively involved in the preservation of Charleston's rich cultural heritage. She is a columnist for the *Charleston Mercury* and has published through McGraw Hill and The History Press. She has also published in *Carologue*, a publication of the South Carolina Historical Society. For many years, she was a professional guide at Winterthur Museum in Delaware and was a partner in an international consulting business that specialized in safety documentation in highly hazardous industries. In Charleston, she has lectured on various topics related to the Holy City's architectural history. She attends the Huguenot Church and is a member of several local organizations and national hereditary societies. She has two fine sons, three grandsons, and three granddaughters of whom she is inordinately proud.

Robert P. Stockton

Born in Biloxi, Bob Stockton adopted Charleston as his home. He is the author of *The Great Shock* and *The History of the Carolina Yacht Club*, and contributed articles to scholarly journals. He wrote *The News and Courier* column "Do you Know Your Charleston" for many years. The column received the South Carolina Chapter of the American Institute of Architects Press Award in 1976. He twice edited the *Notes for Guides of Historic Charleston*. He served on the city's Board of Architectural Review. He is a consultant in historical and architectural research, and an adjunct history professor at the College of Charleston. He has an accomplished son, John DeVeaux Stockton, a grandson, and a step-granddaughter.

Peg Eastman and Bob Stockton. Photograph by Richard P. Donohoe.

CPSIA information can be obtained
at www.ICGtesting.com
Printed in the USA
JSHW052342170822
29430JS00003B/18